Psalm 23
A Psalm of David

The Lord is my shepherd, I shall not want.
He makes me to lie down in green pastures.
He leads me beside the still waters.
He restores my soul.
He leads me in the paths of righteousness for His name's sake.
Yea, though I walk through the valley of the shadow of death,
I will fear no evil for you are with me.
Your rod and your staff, they comfort me.
You prepare a table before me in the presence of my enemies.
You anoint my head with oil, my cup runs over.
Surely goodness and mercy shall follow me all the days of my life,
And I will dwell in the house of the Lord for ever.

Quoted from The Expositor's Study Bible, King James Version,
annotated by Jimmy Swaggart.

D1352767

Oh when the saints
Go marching in
Oh when the saints go marching in
I want to be in that number
When the saints go marching in

Eagle 53
My Ultimate
Musical Tuning

Third Edition
The Mathematics
Behind Eagle 53

John O'Sullivan

Published by
Pan Music Publishing

Copyright © 2021
by John O'Sullivan

Third Edition

ISBN 978-0-9566492-9-4

Contents

To my Family and Friends

Introduction

This book is about an alternative musical tuning that I (with some assistance) have worked out called Eagle 53. The standard tuning in the Western world is called 12 Tone Equal Temperament (12TET for short). With my tuning, Eagle 53, some notes are a bit higher than those in 12TET and others are a bit lower. Eagle 53 has several advantages over 12TET and these are described in this book. There are some mathematical ideas here but they are not overly complicated and most people should be able to grasp them. A prior knowledge of music theory or nomenclature is not required to understand the ideas I propose in this book, which is aimed at the average person.

Here is some of my musical background. When I was around fourteen or fifteen years of age (1984/1985) a guitarist friend of mine showed me how to play the riff from one of my favourite songs: Satisfaction by The Rolling Stones. I got a great thrill out of this simple three note riff and I wanted to learn more. My mother told me she knew someone who gave guitar lessons and I told her I was interested. This person turned out to be none other than Noel Redding, bass guitarist with the Jimi Hendrix Experience.

Noel was a brilliant teacher as well as guitarist (guitar was his main instrument, not the bass). The first thing he taught me was how to tune a guitar. It took me about six weeks to get the hang of tuning. Noel loved fifties rock and roll and he was a big fan of Buddy Holly, Eddie Cochran and The Everly Brothers. Among the first songs I learned from Noel were: C'mon Everybody and Three Steps To Heaven, both by Eddie Cochran. Noel was very particular about tuning his guitar when he played and I think that if he was alive today he would have been interested in my tuning research. He died in 2003 at age 57 and he and his partner Carol Appleby are greatly missed by those who knew them.

After a few years I got to the stage where I could figure out the chords of simple songs by ear (albeit slowly). My guitarist friends would show me how to play more complicated pieces such as Stairway to Heaven by Led Zeppelin. I learned how to read guitar tablature but I can't read standard music notation. I don't know much about western music theory, compositional techniques and such. Overall, I know a few chords and I can improvise a little bit with the pentatonic minor scale and that's about it.

As regards alternative tunings (microtonality) there are literally thousands of alternative tunings documented on the internet (search Scala Archive). There is also a wealth of information and mathematical tuning ideas on the internet but I'm sorry to say I don't quite understand most of it. Luckily I think I don't need to understand it because my own system addresses all my tuning needs. Some people reading this book will be interested in these other methods and ideas and if you are curious check out some of the Facebook tuning groups. Two of them are The Xenharmonic Alliance, and, Microtonal Music and Tuning Theory. The URLs for these are...
www.facebook.com/groups/xenharmonic2
www.facebook.com/groups/497105067092502

In 1995 (aged 25) I read in a book called Engineering Physics that two musical tones played simultaneously sound sweet if the frequencies of the tones correspond to a simple ratio. I was intrigued by this and decided to examine the standard Western tuning (12TET) to see what simple ratios could be found there. I was very surprised to discover that most of the intervals (an interval consists of two musical tones and the distance in pitch or frequency between them) that occur in 12TET are noticeably out of tune. I suspect that most Western musicians aren't aware of the fact that the music they play (in 12TET) is not perfectly in tune and that alternative tunings exist. I set out to find a new and better tuning and after twenty one years of research, and with a little bit of help, I have one: Eagle 53.

I don't remember much about the first few years of my research (beginning in 1995) but at one point I rediscovered quarter comma meantone tuning which is one of the most well known alternative tunings. Around this time I acquired a copy of

David B. Doty's The Just Intonation Primer from which I gleaned some useful information.

In 1998 I went back to school, to the Cork Institute of Technology, to study computer science. There I learned how to write computer programs using C++, a programming language. The ability to program had a huge effect on my research and I was able to investigate ideas that needed thousands, and sometimes millions, of calculations to prove or disprove.

Fast forward to 2009 when I came up with my Blue JI just tuning. J.I. stands for Just Intonation. In any *just* interval the frequencies of the two notes corresponds exactly to an integer ratio, x/y, and the smaller the values of x and y the sweeter the sound, For example two frequencies of 220Hz and 330Hz correspond to 2/3 (220/330 = 2/3) and two tones with these frequencies sound sweet when played together. 220Hz means 220 waves per second.

Blue JI tuning looks like...

1/1 , 15/14, 9/8, 6/5, 5/4, 4/3, 7/5, 3/2, 8/5, 5/3, 9/5, 15/8, 2/1.

If these numbers are meaningless to the reader don't worry, they will be explained later in the book. At that time I was concerned with symmetry which I thought was essential (I don't now). In Blue JI and Blue Temperament (see below) the notes going up from 1/1 are the exact mirror image of the notes going down from 7/5.

I had a list of (what I considered to be) *good* harmony intervals an octave (2/1) or less wide. I wrote a program which raised some notes (in my Blue JI tuning) slightly and lowered other notes slightly in such a way that the number of good harmony intervals that occurred overall was at a maximum. Most of these intervals were not perfectly in tune but close enough to perfect to be acceptable. I called the new tuning Blue Temperament. The word *temperament* implies that at least one interval in a tuning is not just (or perfectly in tune). I thought at the time that this tuning, Blue Temperament, could possibly be the "ultimate" tuning that I was looking for.

Early in 2012 I came up with a new tuning I called Raven Temperament. This scale is not symmetrical but it contains at least one instance of each of the harmony intervals an octave or less wide that I considered to be good at that time. The just version of Raven Temperament looked like this...

1/1, 16/15, 9/8, 6/5, 5/4, 4/3, 7/5, 3/2, 8/5, 5/3, 7/4, 15/8, 2/1.

One of the programs I wrote to temper this just scale (so as to have the maximum number of good harmony intervals) took more than eight hours to run, millions of calculations.

Up until early 2016 Raven Temperament (version 2) was my "ultimate" tuning, mainly because melodically it is strong and it contains a lot (possibly a maximum) of good harmony intervals over a one octave range.

In 2016 I started working on a new tuning. I wanted it to be strong melodically and have at least one strong chord associated with each note. First I came up with a just scale (which it turns out is not new) and this looks like...

1/1, 16/15, 9/8, 6/5, 5/4, 4/3, 7/5, 3/2, 8/5, 5/3, 9/5, 15/8, 2/1.

These numbers will be explained later. I'm calling this scale Eagle JI (JI stands for just intonation). I intended to temper this scale to get a strong chord on each note and this is where I needed some help. I posted the just scale above on an internet tuning forum and one prominent member of the group, Paul Erlich, suggested "tempering out the marvel comma: 225/224". If you don't know what this means don't worry, I don't fully understand it either but at this point I don't need to. Jake Freivald (another member of the same group) had the same idea and proposed three

EDOs (Equal Divisions of the Octave, I'll explain EDOs later) that "temper out" 225/224. These were 41EDO, 53EDO and 72EDO. I looked at the three tunings and 53EDO (specifically a twelve note subset of 53EDO) suited my needs best. It did everything I wanted it to do with incredible accuracy, very near just. I think that this tuning is my "Holy Grail" tuning and it is what I set out to find back in 1995. I call this tuning Eagle 53, or just Eagle. I still have more research to do on harmony and chords but as regards Eagle tuning, I doubt I could improve on it according my current criteria. I settled on Eagle 53 on June 22nd, 2016.

I was told by Manuel Op de Coul (another member of the alternative tuning community) that Eagle 53 is not new. He says it is a 53EDO version of Euler's Genus diatonico-chromaticum (which I think is identical to Eagle J.I. except that Euler used 45/32 instead of Eagle's 7/5) that was already documented before I came up with Eagle 53. I'm not sure. Eagle JI is not new and 53EDO is not new but the intersection of the two might be. I have never seen a mention of the exact 12 notes of Eagle 53 documented anywhere before June 2016.

Either way it doesn't matter too much to me if I am not the first to arrive at this tuning just so long as I know what that tuning is and why it's so good.

There are around thirty musical compositions on my web site, mostly by Chris Vaisvil, that use my older Blue and Raven tunings and a few tunes in Eagle 53 are there as well. The address is...

www.johnsmusic7.com

This book is very short. If I were to write about the hundreds of conjectures I have had in the past (around 80% to 90% of which turned out to be false) and the methods I used to prove/disprove them this book would be over a thousand pages long. I'm just writing about the few nuggets of gold I found after sifting through tons of silt. Many times I have compiled long lists

5

of intervals (computer generated) and then spent ages sorting them in order of strength and/or order of width for the purpose of proving or disproving an idea. A lot of my ideas are not so much "it must be this" but rather "it can't be anything else".

When I began learning the guitar I made a wrong assumption that a lot of novice musicians and many people in general make: that *major* means strong or happy and *minor* means weak or sad. Sure enough major chords sound stronger than minor chords. This however is not technically correct and strictly speaking major/minor refers to the width of certain intervals. A major second (9/8) is wider than a minor second (16/15). A major third (5/4) is wide than a minor third (6/5) and so on. Some people have objected to my "misuse" of these terms so instead of using the term *major* I will use *high strength*. Instead of *minor* I will use *medium strength*. Intervals that are extremely weak are *low strength* intervals and I deem these to be illegal.

Even if my formulas for quantifying the strength values of melody and harmony intervals turn out to be wrong, I think that, for my intents and purposes, the Eagle 53 tuning is unbeatable. This tuning is what I set out to find in 1995 and is the pinnacle of my research.

Eagle 53 is suitable for pianos and MIDI keyboards that can be retuned with the right software. By coincidence Eagle 53 has 12 notes per octave (same as 12TET) so any regular MIDI retunable keyboard could implement Eagle. It is also suitable for stringed and fretted instruments such as guitars or mandolins but the old frets need to be replaced with new frets in new positions, see the chapter called Eagle 53 Guitar.

The ideas I present in this book are according to my current understanding which may be wrong and may change in the future.

Finally, Eagle 53 is what works for *me* and what floats my boat and ticks all my boxes and I'm not *forcing* it upon you, the reader, or anyone else. Pretty much all of the people I have corresponded with in the tuning community that have looked at Eagle 53 want different things and prefer other tunings and that's their prerogative and that's fine by me.

Chapter One
Intervals

An interval could be described as the distance between two musical tones. As I said in the introduction two tones will sound sweet (either played in sequence or simultaneously) if their frequencies correspond to a simple ratio. For example one of the A keys on a piano has a frequency of 220Hz (i.e. 220 waves per second) and the nearest E key above it has a frequency of approximately (but not exactly) 330Hz. Both 220 and 330 are evenly divisible by 110 so 220/330 can be *reduced* to 2/3 when both numbers are divided by 110. The 2 and 3 in 2/3 are small numbers and, in general, the smaller the numbers in the ratio, the sweeter the sound. The convention for writing musical intervals (as ratios) is such that the left hand side (numerator) is equal to or greater than the right hand side (denominator) so that the greater the magnitude of the ratio the wider the interval. So the 2/3 ratio above is usually written as 3/2.

A pair of notes whose frequencies correspond exactly to an integer ratio (e.g. 9/7) is called a *just* interval. Other intervals (e.g. pi/2) are not just, you could call them *irrational* intervals. You could also call them *tempered* intervals if they are approximations of a just interval.

In 12 Tone Equal Temperament the distance between any two adjacent notes is always the same and this distance is called a semitone which is approximately (but not exactly) 18/17. Every note, in 12TET has a frequency of approximately 1.059 times the frequency of the note just below it. There are 100 cents in a semitone (i.e. 100 equal divisions of a semitone called cents) and there are 1200 cents in an octave (an octave. expressed as a ratio, is 2/1, which is twelve semitones, 12 x 100 cents = 1200 cents). A perfect fifth (3/2) in 12TET is 700 cents but this is not perfectly in tune, it is slightly flat of just. In just intonation a perfect fifth (3/2) is 701.955 cents.

The 'oct' in 'octave' relates to the fact that 2/1 is the *eighth* note in the major scale (described below). The perfect fifth corresponds to the fifth note in the major scale and the perfect fourth (500 cents in 12TET, this is slightly wider than a just 4/3 by approximately 2 cents) corresponds to the fourth note in the major scale. The major scale, justly tuned, looks like this:

1/1, 9/8, 5/4, 4/3, 3/2, 5/3, 15/8, 2/1.

These notes correspond to: do re mi fa so la ti do. Each note (expressed as ratios, x/y, above) in this scale shows how it relates to the first note: 1/1. So 9/8 indicates a note that is 9/8 (1.125) times higher in frequency than 1/1. 5/4 is a note that is 5/4 (1.25) times higher than 1/1. And so on. The 1/1 could correspond to any desired frequency.

The notes in Eagle JI (JI stands for just intonation) are...

1/1, 16/15, 9/8, 6/5, 5/4, 4/3, 7/5, 3/2, 8/5, 5/3, 9/5, 15/8, 2/1.

All the notes between 1/1 and 2/1 are tempered (raised or lowered) slightly to yield my Eagle 53 tuning. In Eagle 53, apart from the tritone (7/5), all the notes between 1/1 and 2/1 are tempered up or down by less than 1.6 cents which means that these notes are *very* close to just, or pure.

There are lists of what I deem to be *good* melody (two notes played in sequence) and harmony (two notes played simultaneously) intervals in the chapters on melody and harmony respectively.

Chapter Two
The Harmonic Series
and Periodicity

Most musical instruments (e.g. guitar, organ, piano) produce musical tones that have a harmonic series or overtones. To illustrate, when a guitar string is played there is more than one frequency produced. The loudest and lowest frequency is called the fundamental or first harmonic. The next frequency is called the second harmonic, or first overtone, and has a frequency twice that of the fundamental and a loudness or intensity half that of the fundamental. The next frequency is called the third harmonic, or second overtone, and has a frequency three times that of the fundamental and a loudness or intensity one third that of the fundamental and so on. The waves on the string occur simultaneously and look like this...

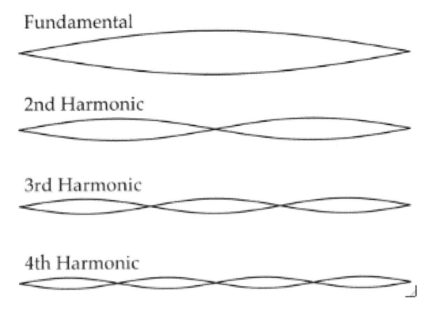

Fundamental

2nd Harmonic

3rd Harmonic

4th Harmonic

In practice the frequencies of the second and subsequent harmonics (also called overtones) may be slightly higher than 2x,

3x, 4x, 5x etc. (the fundamental frequency is x) and the difference varies from instrument to instrument but I assume perfect harmonicity for the purpose of working out a tuning.

Other instruments (e.g. bells) do not produce a regular harmonic series like the one described above. It could be the case that a harmony interval that sounds good on an instrument with a regular harmonic series might sound unacceptable on an instrument with a different set of overtones or vice-versa.

Early in my research it occurred to me that the overtones of notes needed to be considered as well as the fundamentals when working out the strength values of intervals. After looking in to it I think if the timbre is fairly harmonic (like the guitar string on the previous page) then only the fundamentals need to be considered.

In this book, when I say "a regular harmonic series" or "regular timbre" I am talking about a set of overtones similar to the one described on the previous page.

Periodicity

Periodicity is another important concept. When the sound wave patterns of the fundamentals of two notes that correspond to a simple just interval are plotted on a graph the pattern repeats itself at certain points that are all the same distance apart. In the graph below the fundamentals of the 3/2 interval are plotted and the arrows indicate the repeat points...

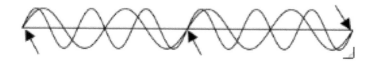

The lower the numbers in the interval ratio the better is the periodicity. If you plot the first, say 16 harmonics or overtones of each note then the repeat points will still be in the same positions.

Consider a four note major chord with frequencies of 400

Hz, 500 Hz, 600 Hz and 800 Hz. The smallest integers that represent the chord are: 4:5:6:8. So each repeat point occurs after 4 cycles of the first note, 5 cycles of the second note, 6 cycles of the third note and 8 cycles of the fourth note.

Now consider a minor chord with frequencies of 400 Hz, 480 Hz, 600 Hz and 800 Hz. The smallest integers that represent the chord are: 10:12:15:20, larger numbers indicating poorer periodicity.

When calculating the strength values of chords it is wrong to isolate each of the intervals that occur in the chord and simplify them. To illustrate... in the 4:5:6:8 chord you have 4:5, 4:6 (simplifies to 2:3), 4:8, (simplifies to 1:2), 5:6, 5:8 and 6:8 (simplifies to 3:4). In the 10:12:15:20 chord you have 10:12 (simplifies to 5:6), 10:15 (simplifies to 2:3), 10:20 (simplifies to 1:2), 12:15 (simplifies to 4:5), 12:20 (simplifies to 3:5), 15:20 (simplifies to 3:4).

When all the intervals in each chord are simplified they all have the same intervals in common except that the 4:5:6:8 chord has a 5:8 interval and the 10:12:15:20 chord has a 3:5 interval. 3:5 is stronger than 5:8 so one would think that the 10:12:15:20 chord should be stronger than the 4:5:6:8 chord but on listening the opposite is true. So for calculating chord strength it is much less important to isolate pairs of notes (intervals) in a chord and simplify them (e.g. 6:8 simplifies to 3:4). Instead all the notes in a chord have to be considered according to the lowest integers that represent the *whole* chord (e.g. a six note minor chord on a justly tuned guitar is 10:15:20:24:30:40) when working out the overall strength of the chord.

The frequencies of the notes (and how they relate to each other) in an open E major chord on a guitar (justly tuned) could be represented by the following integers: 2:3:4:5:6:8. All small numbers indicating good periodicity. Now change the G sharp note to a G to get an E minor chord and the new lowest integer representation of the chord is: 10:15:20:24:30:40. Much higher numbers and therefore much poorer periodicity.

Chapter Three
12 Tone Equal Temperament

Below is a section of a piano keyboard. The white keys are named A, B, C, D, E, F, G and this pattern repeats as you go left or right. The distance between one A key and the next, going left or right is called an octave and as a ratio is written 2/1. The same is true for all the other eleven keys: A sharp (A#), B, C, C sharp (C#), D etc. The black key between C and D is called C sharp (C#) or D flat (Db). The black key between F and G is called F sharp (F#) or G flat (Gb), and so on. Equal temperament got its name from the fact that the distance between any two adjacent notes (a semitone) is always the same. As I said earlier there are 100 cents in a semitone and expressed as a ratio a semitone is approximately, but not exactly, 18/17.

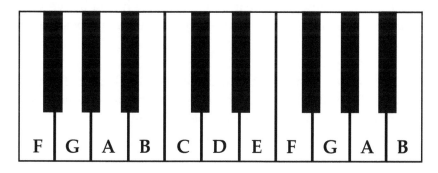

When creating a tuning or scale it is usual and convenient to establish a certain number of notes over a one octave range (i.e. between 1/1 and 2/1) and then to *mirror* these notes in lower and higher octaves. Say we choose the following notes over a one octave range: 1/1, 6/5, 5/4, 4/3, 3/2, 8/5, 5/3, 9/5 and 2/1. In the octave *below* 1/1 we halve each note to get 1/2, 3/5, 5/8, 2/3, 3/4, 4/5, 5/6, 9/10 and 1/1. In the octave *above* 2/1 we double each note to get: 2/1, 12/5, 5/2, 8/3, 3/1, 16/5, 10/3, 18/5 and 4/1. And so on. This is called 'octave repeating'.

Before I explain how 12TET came into being let's look at the earliest tuning I know of (Pythagorean tuning). It looks like this...

$$1/1, \quad 9/8, \quad 81/64, \quad 4/3, \quad 3/2, \quad 27/16, \quad 243/128, \quad 2/1$$

The strongest note between 1/1 and 2/1, paired with 1/1, is 3/2. It would be nice if every note had a note above it and below it so as to make a 3/2 interval. Here is my understanding of what Pythagoras did to create this scale. He started with 1/1 and 2/1. He multiplied 1/1 by 3/2 to get 3/2. next he multiplied 3/2 by 3/2 to get 9/4. This is outside of the one octave range (i.e. greater than 2/1) so he halved the note to get 9/8 (one octave lower than 9/4) which is between 1/1 and 2/1. Next he multiplied 9/8 by 3/2 to get 27/16. He multiplied 27/16 by 3/2 to get 81/32 which is outside of the one octave range (i.e. greater than 2/1). So he halved the note to get 81/64 (one octave lower than 81/32). He multiplied 81/64 by 3/2 to get 243/128 and now we have the scale shown just above this paragraph. Most, but not all, of the notes have a note 3/2 times higher above them and a note 2/3 times lower below them if the scale repeats every octave.

This scale was created using a *chain* of Perfect Fifths (a Perfect Fifth is 3/2). Using chains of intervals, whether using fifths or other intervals, just or tempered, is an important part of microtonal (alternative tuning) theory.

The Pythagorean scale above is a *just* scale because the good intervals that occur correspond exactly to integer ratios. This tuning is a 3 *prime limit* tuning because 3 is the highest prime factor that occurs among the numbers in the intervals. In other words all of the numbers in the intervals that occur are divisible exactly by the prime numbers 2 or 3, no 5s or 7s or 11s etc.

Most of the notes in Pythagorean tuning have a perfect fifth both above and below them.

Ptolemy improved on this and his tuning was...

$$1/1, \quad 9/8, \quad 5/4, \quad 4/3, \quad 3/2, \quad 5/3, \quad 15/8, \quad 2/1$$

Perhaps what Ptolemy did was simply replace the 81/64 in Pythagoras' scale with 5/4 and replaced 27/16 with 5/3 and replaced 243/128 with 15/8. 5/4 and 5/3 and 15/8 go better with 1/1 than the corresponding notes in the Pythagorean scale.

This is also a just tuning. This tuning is a 5 *prime limit* tuning because 5 is the highest prime factor that occurs among the numbers in the intervals. In 15/8 the highest prime factor of 15 is 5. In other words all of the numbers in the intervals that occur are divisible exactly by the prime numbers 2, 3 or 5, no 7's or 11's or 13's etc.

12 Tone Equal Temperament (12TET) is *not* a just tuning because most of the good intervals that occur are not perfectly in tune. It is a compromise system. Here's my understanding of how it was developed.

The Origins of 12 Tone Equal Temperament

Start with 1/1 and 2/1 and then add some notes in between using the same method as for the Pythagorean scale above (using a chain of just perfect fifths or 3/2s).

Beginning with 1, multiply it by 3/2 to get 1.5. Now multiply 1.5 by 3/2 to get 2.25. 2.25 is outside of the one octave range (i.e. is higher than 2.0) so divide it by 2 to get 1.125. As I said above, notes in lower octaves have frequencies exactly half of those in the higher octaves just above them.

We now have four notes: 1.0, 1.125, 1.5 and 2.0. Now take 1.125 and multiply that by 3/2 to get 1.6875. Multiply 1.6875 by 3/2 to get 2.53125. This is outside of the one octave range (i.e. higher than 2.0) so divide it by 2 to get 1.265625. After 12 iterations you get 1.013643317 which is very close to our starting point of 1.0. At this point, if you ignore the 1.013643317, there are 12 notes per octave and all of them, can be paired with another note either above or below it so that a perfect 3/2 interval occurs (if the scale repeats every octave).

One major problem with this tuning is that the sixth note (when the notes are arranged in ascending order of frequency), 1.351524353, is very out of tune with the tonic, 1.0. The word *tonic* means the root or key note of a piece of music. Ideally the sixth note should be 1.333333 which is 4/3. 4/3 is called a perfect fourth. So if you are playing a melody using this chain of fifths tuning the perfect fourth will be 23.5 cents out of tune which is unacceptable (my maximum deviation from just is currently 8.474 cents).

It is likely that 12TET was discovered independently by more than one person and the clever idea was to temper (adjust slightly) the 3/2 in the chain of fifths so that the thirteenth note, after 12 iterations, was 1.0 exactly, the same as the starting point. So instead of multiplying each note by 3/2 (which is 1.5 in decimal) you multiply each note by 2.9966/2 (which is 1.4983). Now every perfect fifth (3/2) that occurs is only 2 cents out of tune which is very acceptable and every perfect fourth (4/3) is now also only 2 cents out of tune. Because the thirteenth note in the chain of tempered fifths is the same as the first note the chain of fifths is called a *circle* of fifths. Now every note has a perfect fifth and a perfect fourth both above and below them and these are only 2 cents out of tune which is excellent.

Where did 2.9966 come from? Without going in to too much detail what you have is a chain of twos roughly equal to a chain of threes. 3 to the power of 12 is 531441 and 2 to the power of 19 is 524288. 531441 is roughly equal to 524288. The twelfth root of 524288 is 2.9966 which is very close to 3.0. So a chain of 2.9966/2s (or 1.4983) will form a circle of 12 notes per octave, all the same distance apart with good fourths and fifths everywhere.

531441/524288 is called the Pythagorean *comma* and you will often hear microtonalists talk about tempering out commas and there are a lot of different commas used out there.

So that's my understanding of the origin of 12 Tone Equal Temperament. Below is a list of intervals that occur in 12TET. The first column shows the widths (in cents) of the 12TET intervals over a one octave range. The second column shows the names of the intervals. The third column shows the ideal just intervals (corresponding to Eagle JI) near the 12TET intervals and the fourth column shows the widths of the *just* intervals in cents. Aug is short for augmented and dim is short for diminished.

```
     Intervals  in  12  Tone  Equal  Temperament
                 and  Eagle  JI


   0c   Unison/Tonic                   1/1      0.0c
 100c   Minor Second                  16/15   111.7c
 200c   Major Second                   9/8    203.9c
 300c   Minor Third                    6/5    315.6c
 400c   Major Third                    5/4    386.3c
 500c   Perfect Fourth                 4/3    498.0c
 600c   Aug Fourth/Dim Fifth           7/5    582.5c
 700c   Perfect Fifth                  3/2    702.0c
 800c   Aug Fifth/Minor Sixth          8/5    813.7c
 900c   Major Sixth/Dim Seventh        5/3    884.4c
1000c   Minor Seventh                  9/5   1017.6c
1100c   Major Seventh                 15/8   1088.3c
1200c   Octave                         2/1   1200.0c
```

I don't use chains of intervals in my system because you can't do what I do using them. The only advantage I can see with chains of intervals is that you can modulate (change key) and many of the notes in a chains tuning can be used as a tonic (key note).

The pros and cons of 12TET

Because the distance between any two adjacent notes is always the same (a semitone or 100 cents) you can choose any key you want as the tonic of a piece of music and it will be just as good as any other key. You can also play all of the good chords available (major, minor, seventh etc.) in all keys. Also all of the strongest intervals, over a one octave range, occur (i.e. 1/1, 4/3, 3/2, 2/1) and are all within 2 cents accuracy which is very good.

The downside is that there are very few good harmony intervals that are within plus or minus 8.474 cents accuracy of just (see the chapter on tempering tolerance). The only good harmony intervals that occur within +/-8.474 cents accuracy, over a one octave range, are: 1/1, 9/8, 4/3, 3/2 and 2/1. So the following harmony intervals are more than 8.474 cents out of tune...

8/7, 7/6, 6/5, 5/4, 9/7, 11/8, 7/5, 10/7, 11/7, 8/5, 13/8, 5/3, 12/7, 7/4, 9/5, 11/6 and 13/7.

Many of these good intervals are more than 20 cents out of tune in 12TET making them completely unusable (in 12TET). It would be nice to have a tuning system that contains *all* of the above harmony intervals (at least over a one octave range and all within 8.474 cents accuracy). My older Raven Temperament (v2) tuning, was designed for (using a 6.7758 cents tolerance), and has, this property (I need to check if 13/8 is good in Raven v2). Eagle 53 doesn't have this property. The 11/9, 11/8, 11/7, 11/6 and 13/8 intervals don't occur within 8.474 cents accuracy in Eagle 53. I don't miss these intervals because notes containing primes of 11 or 13 or higher generally don't pair well with many other notes in a 12 note per octave tuning where most of the notes are 5 or 7 limit when paired with 1/1 or 2/1. The lower the prime limits of the intervals (in a tuning) in general, the more strong intervals occur.

Chapter Four
Other Alternative Tunings

Quarter-Comma Meantone Temperament

I think that the most famous western tuning apart from 12TET is Quarter-Comma Meantone Temperament. The comma used here is 81/80, the syntonic comma. The fourth root of 80 is 2.990697562 (close to 3) and this is used in the chain of fifths (i.e. 2.990697562/2 which is 1.495348781). With this tuning most of the perfect fifths are out of tune by 5.4 cents which is acceptable and most of the major thirds (5/4) are perfectly in tune. The chain however does not make a circle but rather an infinite spiral that never exactly reaches the starting point of 1.0. You can also divide each note by 2.990697562/2 (i.e. go in the other direction). Notes could be chosen in a variety of ways. For example you could choose 10, 11 or 12 iterations going up and none going down, 7 iterations going up and 5 going down, etc. Any number of iterations can be chosen, going up and/or down.

I discovered Quarter Comma Meantone myself before I read about it. In my version I started with a tonic D and I used a chain of eight tempered fifths going up and eight going down from 1/1, yielding 17 notes per octave. The notes were named: D, D#, Eb, E, F, F#, Gb, G, G#, Ab, A, A#, Bb, B, C, C#, Db. (# means sharp and b means flat). In this scale D# is lower than Eb, F# is lower than Gb and so on. I refretted a guitar to implement this scale and all the frets were continuous across the neck (i.e. not staggered like the fretboard on the back cover of this book). On this guitar a few D#s occur here and there and a few Ebs occur elsewhere instead. A few F#s occur here and there and a few Gbs occur elsewhere instead. This meantone guitar was interesting to look at but not very versatile.

EDOs

EDO stands for Equal Division of the Octave. 12 Tone Equal Temperament could also be called 12EDO (12 equal divisions of the octave) because the octave is divided into twelve equal steps. Other EDOs are well known in tuning circles. Some of the more popular low numbered EDOs are 17, 19, 22, 24 and 31 equal divisions of the octave. 17EDO has good fourths and fifths (within 8.474 cents accuracy). 22EDO has some interesting chords.

Before I arrived at Eagle 53 one of my favourite tunings was a twelve note subset of 31EDO which I call Credo (a contraction of Crow + edo = Credo). Here are the notes of Credo in cents...

0.0, 116.129, 193.5484, 309.6774, 387.0968, 503.2258, 580.6452, 696.7742, 812.9032, 890.3226, 1006.4516, 1083.871, 1200.0.

If the notes are named similarly to 12TET and E is the tonic then the E major, A major and B major chords are all good within 8.474 cents accuracy. That is: a major chord on 1/1, 4/3 and 3/2. If the tonic is C then the C major, F major and G major chords are all good. Using conventional terminology the I, IV and V chords are available.

You could have equal divisions of any number. xED3 (x equal divisions of 3/1) scales are also fairly well known in tuning circles. Some people use phi and pi and e and other fundamental constants in their tunings but I don't think that they are practical.

If I had to choose an EDO where *all* the notes are fretted on a guitar it would be 19EDO. This is the smallest EDO where the 2:3:4:5:6:8 major chord is within 7.3 cents of just or pure. Also every interval in 19EDO (in a melodic context) over *any* range (e.g. seven octaves) is good (for me) except for the single step 63 cents interval.

22EDO is interesting as well but it doesn't have 2:3:4:5:6:8 major chords within 8.474 cents of just. On a guitar I won't go higher than 22 frets per octave. I don't care for 24EDO. Some people like guitars fretted for 31EDO but 31 is way too many notes for me. The frets on a 31EDO guitar will be too close to each other for comfortable playing, for me at least, and the complexity is high.

Harmonic Series Tunings

These are tunings that are a portion of the harmonic series. Here are some popular ones...

8:9:10:11:12:13:14:15:16

12:13:14:15:16:17:18:19:20:21:22:23:24

16 to 32 and 24 to 48 are sometimes used as well. Prime numbers higher than 7 (and their multiples, e.g. 11 and 22 and 33) could be omitted to tidy things up a bit.

Chapter Five
Melody and Scales

A large part of my system is based on educated guesses. Here's the first and most important guess. I started with melody (notes played in sequence) because it's simpler than harmony (notes played simultaneously). In harmony a phenomenon called beating occurs which has an unpleasant sound but beating does not occur in melody.

When playing any two notes in sequence the melodic progression from one to the other will sound sweet if the frequencies of the notes correspond to a simple ratio (e.g. 3/2). In general, the smaller the numbers in the ratio the sweeter the progression. Based on this fact I thought that there should be a mathematical formula that quantifies how sweet a melodic interval is.

If the ratio is written as x/y and x and y are both integers and x is greater than or equal to y then a few guesses for a mathematical formula I had were: $1/xy$ or $1/(x+y)$ or $1/x + 1/y$ or $1/x$. These are reasonable guesses because the lower the values of x and y, the greater the result. The last formula, $1/x$, doesn't feature the 'y'. Just as a chain is only as strong as its weakest link then maybe an interval is only as strong as the inverse of the larger number in the ratio.

To test each formula I chose around a dozen or more simple intervals (e.g. 5/3, 5/4, 6/5, 7/4, 7/5, 7/6 etc.) and arranged them in decreasing order of strength according to each formula except the $1/xy$ formula as I considered it unlikely. So I had three lists of intervals and these were all ordered differently according to each of the three formulas (e.g. one formula indicated that interval 'a' was stronger than interval 'b' and another formula indicated the opposite).

I found testing some of the intervals (playing two notes in

sequence whose frequencies corresponded to the intervals in the lists) very difficult. I found that I would decide that interval 'c' sounded stronger than interval 'd' but would come back an hour later and think that the opposite was true. I couldn't be sure.

So first I listened for *strength* and in some cases I couldn't make up my mind as to which of two intervals was stronger. Next I listened for *sweetness* and the same uncertainty occurred. Then I listened for *resolution* (if you play in the key of E then the B note will sound more *resolved* than the B flat note) and I still couldn't be sure. Finally I remembered reading in Ralph Denyer's The Guitar Handbook that the octave (2/1) sounds almost like the *same note* as the tonic (1/1). So then I tried listening for *similarity* and suddenly everything fell into place and the testing became very easy. With all the melodic intervals I tested the lower note was the same note, or frequency, let's say it was called x. If the higher note in the first interval tested sounded *more similar* to x than the higher note in the second interval tested then the first melodic interval should be stronger.

Wait a second, does similarity automatically correspond to strength, sweetness and resolution? Are they all the same thing or are they four different qualities? I'm not sure but I think it is highly unlikely that they are different qualities. So I'm guessing that similarity *does* correspond to strength, sweetness and resolution.

In the end the $1/x + 1/y$ formula was clearly the most likely candidate and the order of intervals for this formula was very consistent with what my ears were telling me. Just to be sure I had a quick look at the $1/xy$ formula which I had not tested yet. I found one clear inconsistency and so ruled it out.

I can't 100% guarantee that $1/x + 1/y$ is the correct formula for melody but after long testing and years of use I have never come across something that would contradict it.

When testing these melodic intervals I used sine wave tones which have a fundamental but no overtones (or higher harmonics). I thought that using musical tones with a regular harmonic series (see chapter two) might produce different results. Later I wrote a program using the $1/x + 1/y$ formula that took into consideration the first 1024 harmonics or overtones of both notes in melodic intervals and though the magnitudes of the results were much higher, the proportions were exactly the same (i.e. the order of strengths for the intervals with a regular harmonic series was the exact same as for sine wave tones). In other words the formula $1/x + 1/y$ seemed to apply to both sine wave tones and tones with a regular harmonic series as described in chapter two.

So which melodic intervals are good and which are bad? I found that (using my $1/x + 1/y$ formula) any melodic interval with a value greater than 0.5 (e.g. 5/3 has a value of $1/5 + 1/3 = 0.5333$) sounded like a high strength melodic interval. I thought that a melodic interval with a value between 0.125 and 0.5 sounds like a medium strength interval. And I thought that a melodic interval with a value less than 0.125 (using either sine wave tones or regular tones) was a low strength (very weak, perhaps so weak as to be illegal) melodic interval.

Later, to line up with my ideas on harmony intervals, I changed the cut-off point from 0.125 to 0.1 (using the $1/x + 1/y$ formula. So a melodic interval with a value less than 0.1 (using the $1/x + 1/y$ formula) is a low strength interval, extremely weak and is, for me, illegal.

At one point I decided to 'pretty up' the formula and change it to $2/x + 2/y$ so that the cut off point for a high strength melodic interval was 1.0 instead of 0.5. Why? In harmony I think that any two notes played simultaneously that sound stronger than either note played on its own is a high strength interval and any pair of notes played simultaneously that sounds weaker than either note in the interval played on it's own is a medium or low strength interval. Each note on its own I assign a strength value of 1.0. I wanted my melody formula to behave the same way as my harmony formula (i.e. a result of 1.0 or higher indicates a high strength interval and less than 1.0 indicates a medium or low

24

strength interval). To get these results I changed the formula from $1/x + 1/y$ to $2/x + 2/y$. Changing the formula from $1/x + 1/y$ to $2/x + 2/y$ will annoy some but essentially the order of melodic intervals will be exactly the same using either formula. Maybe because two notes are involved in an interval then the $1/x + 1/y$ formula should be doubled to $2/x + 2/y$. I have yet to find a simple just interval that contradicts my formula and the rationale behind it.

To recapitulate here I propose three classifications of just melodic intervals...

(i) A melodic interval with a value greater than or equal to 1.0 (using the $2/x + 2/y$ formula) is a High Strength melodic interval.

(ii) A melodic interval with a value between 0.2 and 0.9999 inclusive (using the $2/x + 2/y$ formula) is a Medium Strength melodic interval. I chose the 0.2 threshold because it is half of the threshold for a *good* harmony interval (0.4). This is an educated guess backed up with some listening tests.

(iii) A melodic interval with a value less than 0.2 (using the $2/x + 2/y$ formula) is a Low Strength (very weak) melodic interval and I won't use it.

There are two melody intervals in 12TET (between $1/1$ and $2/1$) that I deem to be low strength and therefore illegal. These are the major third (400 cents in 12TET) and the major sixth (900 cents in 12 TET). The closest legal (for me) melodic intervals to 400 cents are 5/4 (386.3c) and 19/15 (409.2c). 400c is more than 8.474 cents away from both so 400c is for me an illegal melodic interval.

The closest legal (for me) melodic intervals to 900 cents are 5/3 (884.4c) and 22/13 (910.8c). 900c is more than 8.474 cents from both so 900c is for me an illegal melodic interval. See the list of legal melodic intervals beginning on the next page.

Now that I think about it, if you are not too fussy about

the tiny amount of excess cents difference mentioned above, 12TET, using all 13 notes over a one octave range (between 1/1 and 2/1 inclusive), is very close to being a *hyper scale* (in a hyper scale *all* of the notes used between 1/1 and 2/1 inclusive make high or medium strength melodic interval when paired with each other within 8.474 cents accuracy, more on hyper scales later).

In Eagle JI and Eagle 53 every note, over a one octave range (between 1/1 and 2/1), when paired with either 1/1 or 2/1 will be within 6.7758 cents (my older tuning tolerance, 256/255, a bit stricter than my current tolerance, 8.474 cents) of a high strength or medium strength melodic interval, no low strength melodic intervals occur in this set. Low strength intervals do occur elsewhere between 9/8 and 5/3, 6/5 and 5/4, 8/5 and 5/3, 9/5 and 15/8, 7/5 and 32/15, and, 9/5 and 8/3 and I avoid them.

Below is a list of 87 high strength and medium strength melodic intervals over a one octave range arranged in order of width. This list is not insignificant, for me it serves as a *map* for working out new tuning systems. I like to have all the notes in a given tuning (between 1/1 and 2/1) to be high or medium strength melodically when paired with *both* the tonic (1/1) *and* the octave (2/1) within an accuracy of plus or minus 8.474 cents. The ratios on the left are the just melodic intervals, the numbers in the middle column are the strength values of the intervals using the 2/x + 2/y formula (all values are greater than or equal to 0.2). The numbers on the right are the widths of the intervals in cents.

1/1	4	0.0000
20/19	0.2053	88.8007
19/18	0.2164	93.6030
18/17	0.2288	98.9546
17/16	0.2426	104.9554
16/15	0.2583	111.7313
15/14	0.2762	119.4428
14/13	0.2967	128.2982
13/12	0.3205	138.5727
12/11	0.3485	150.6371
11/10	0.3818	165.0042

21/19	0.2005	173.2679
10/9	0.4222	182.4037
19/17	0.2229	192.5576
9/8	0.4722	203.9100
17/15	0.2510	216.6867
8/7	0.5357	231.1741
15/13	0.2872	247.7411
7/6	0.6190	266.8709
20/17	0.2176	281.3583
13/11	0.3357	289.2097
19/16	0.2303	297.5130
6/5	0.7333	315.6413
17/14	0.2605	336.1295
11/9	0.4040	347.4079
16/13	0.2788	359.4723
21/17	0.2129	365.8255
5/4	0.9000	386.3137
19/15	0.2386	409.2443
14/11	0.3247	417.5080
9/7	0.5079	435.0841
22/17	0.2086	446.3625
13/10	0.3538	454.2140
17/13	0.2715	464.4278
21/16	0.2202	470.7809
4/3	1.1667	498.0450
23/17	0.2046	523.3189
19/14	0.2481	528.6871
15/11	0.3152	536.9508
11/8	0.4318	551.3179
18/13	0.2650	563.3823
7/5	0.6857	582.5122
24/17	0.2010	596.9996
17/12	0.2843	603.0004
10/7	0.4857	617.4878
23/16	0.2120	628.2744
13/9	0.3761	636.6177
16/11	0.3068	648.6821
19/13	0.2591	656.9854
22/15	0.2242	663.0492

```
 3/2    1.6667   701.9550
23/15   0.2203   740.0056
20/13   0.2538   745.7861
17/11   0.2995   753.6375
14/9    0.3651   764.9159
25/16   0.2050   772.6274
11/7    0.4675   782.4920
19/12   0.2719   795.5580
 8/5    0.6500   813.6863
21/13   0.2491   830.2533
13/8    0.4038   840.5277
18/11   0.2929   852.5921
23/14   0.2298   859.4484
 5/3    1.0667   884.3587
22/13   0.2448   910.7903
17/10   0.3176   918.6417
12/7    0.4524   933.1291
19/11   0.2871   946.1951
26/15   0.2103   952.2590
 7/4    0.7857   968.8259
23/13   0.2408   987.7467
16/9    0.3472   996.0900
25/14   0.2229  1003.8015
 9/5    0.6222  1017.5963
20/11   0.2818  1034.9958
11/6    0.5152  1049.3629
24/13   0.2372  1061.4273
13/7    0.4396  1071.7018
28/15   0.2048  1080.5572
15/8    0.3833  1088.2687
17/9    0.3399  1101.0454
19/10   0.3053  1111.1993
21/11   0.2771  1119.4630
23/12   0.2536  1126.3193
25/13   0.2338  1132.0998
27/14   0.2169  1137.0391
29/15   0.2023  1141.3085
 2/1    3.0000  1200.0000
```

I repeat, any melodic interval within 8.474 cents of any of the good melodic intervals listed above should be good.

Going back to around 2012 or earlier I decided that any seven note per octave scale (eight notes if you count both 1/1 and 2/1) *must* have 1/1, 4/3, 3/2 and 2/1 (just or tempered) and must not have three or more notes bunched up close together as this would be *unbalanced*. There are 30 scales listed in the chapter on Eagle 53 Scales that have these properties.

I think differently now and I use other scales that don't have the properties described in the paragraph above but are strongly rooted instead, more on this later.

For the 30 eight-note scales I mentioned above I started with 1/1, 4/3, 3/2 and 2/1 for each one. I added two notes between 1/1 and 4/3 and two notes between 3/2 and 2/1. In the list of scales below each 1 corresponds to a note used in any given 12 note per octave tuning (e.g. Eagle) and each 0 is a note not used. There are eight 1s and 5 0s in each scale. For the sake of balance I allow no more than two adjacent notes (e.g. 111, three adjacent notes is illegal). The first four scales are symmetrical and the subsequent six pairs of scales are the approximate inverse of each other. The list below applies to any twelve notes per octave tuning where every note is within around twenty cents of the notes in 12TET. I don't know the correct names of all the scales so I named some of them myself according to some place names from The Lord of the Rings and The Silmarillion by J.R.R. Tolkien. The 1s on the left indicate 1/1, the two 1s in the middle separated by a 0 indicate 4/3 and 3/2 and the 1s on the right indicate 2/1.

```
------------------------------------------------
Melodic Major        1 0 1 0 1 1 0 1 1 0 1 0 1
------------------------------------------------
Arabian              1 1 0 0 1 1 0 1 1 0 0 1 1
------------------------------------------------
Dorian               1 0 1 1 0 1 0 1 0 1 1 0 1
------------------------------------------------
Neapolitan Major     1 1 0 1 0 1 0 1 0 1 0 1 1
------------------------------------------------
Major/Ionian         1 0 1 0 1 1 0 1 0 1 0 1 1
Phrygian             1 1 0 1 0 1 0 1 1 0 1 0 1
------------------------------------------------
Mixolydian           1 0 1 0 1 1 0 1 0 1 1 0 1
Natural Minor        1 0 1 1 0 1 0 1 1 0 1 0 1
------------------------------------------------
Gondolin             1 1 0 0 1 1 0 1 0 1 0 1 1
Neapolitan Minor     1 1 0 1 0 1 0 1 1 0 0 1 1
------------------------------------------------
Harmonic Major       1 0 1 0 1 1 0 1 1 0 0 1 1
Numenor              1 1 0 0 1 1 0 1 1 0 1 0 1
------------------------------------------------
Lorien               1 1 0 0 1 1 0 1 0 1 1 0 1
Harmonic Minor       1 0 1 1 0 1 0 1 1 0 0 1 1
------------------------------------------------
Melodic Minor        1 0 1 1 0 1 0 1 0 1 0 1 1
Rivendell            1 1 0 1 0 1 0 1 0 1 1 0 1
------------------------------------------------
```

In Eagle 53 it seems to me that the Dorian scale does not occur as a hyper scale (more on hyper scales later) in any key. All the other fifteen scales do occur as hyper scales.

In the following six-note scales (6 counting both 1/1 and 2/1 and four notes in between) below not more than 2 consecutive spaces occur for the purpose of balance and two adjacent notes do not occur for the purpose of balance.

```
---------------------------------------------------
Oriental              1 0 1 0 0 1 0 1 0 1 0 0 1
---------------------------------------------------
Smooth                1 0 1 0 0 1 0 1 0 0 1 0 1
---------------------------------------------------
Oriental Inverse      1 0 0 1 0 1 0 1 0 1 0 0 1
---------------------------------------------------
Pentatonic Minor      1 0 0 1 0 1 0 1 0 0 1 0 1
---------------------------------------------------
```

Six note scales (counting both 1/1 and 2/1 and the four notes in between) sound good to me but do not have much variety.

See the chapter on composition for building scales or a 'melodic base'.

Hyper Scales

In Eagle 53, if I want to play a major chord on 1/1, 4/3 and 3/2 (the I, IV, V chords) I need the following notes (or scale) and the corresponding notes in lower and higher octaves...

$$1/1, \ 9/8, \ 5/4, \ 4/3, \ 3/2, \ 5/3, \ 15/8, \ 2/1$$

In Eagle 53 all of these notes are within 1.6 cents accuracy of just. I noticed a problem with this scale. 5/3 over 9/8 makes 40/27 which is 680 cents (after tempering to Eagle 53 this turns out to be 679 cents). Looking at the list of good melodic intervals a few pages back 679 cents is not within 8.474 cents of any of the good intervals listed. It is 16 cents wider than 22/15 (663 cents) and 23 cents narrower than 3/2 (702 cents) so it is a Low Strength melodic interval. I like to avoid low strength intervals whenever possible but the I, IV and V chord group (three major chords whose root notes correspond to 6:8:9) is probably the strongest and most used group of chords in the Western world, the foundations of blues and rock, and therefore I allow the scale above but I'm not too happy about it. I call this scale above Major 145 (pronounced Major - one - four - five) because it contains the I, IV and V chords. It is *not* a hyper scale (explained below).

As I said earlier, in Eagle 53 I have identified exactly 30 seven notes per octave scales (all containing 1/1, 4/3, 3/2 and 2/1 and without three or more notes bunched up close together), on 4 different keys, where *every* note, paired with *every other* other note (over a one octave range) makes a melodic interval that is within 8.474 cents of one or more of the good melodic intervals listed a few pages back. These good melodic intervals have values greater than 0.2 using the $2/x + 2/y$ formula. So in these 30 scales *all* of the melodic intervals, over a one octave range are either High Strength or Medium Strength, no Low Strength intervals and therefore these scales should sound very sweet. I call these scales, with no Low Strength intervals (over the one octave range) *Hyper Scales*. In the chapter on Eagle 53 Scales I list these 30 seven notes per octave hyper scales that occur in Eagle 53. However these 30 scales are not strongly rooted (more on this later).

What about the 1/1, 9/8, 5/4, 4/3, 3/2, 5/3, 15/8, 2/1 Major 145 scale above which is not a hyper scale? I can't rule it out because it contains the I, IV, V chords and I won't do without these chords. I could argue that the *root notes* of these major chords (which are 1/1, 4/3 and 3/2) conform to a number of hyper scales and the other notes in the chords perhaps do not matter. In other words, as long as the root notes in any (strongly rooted, see page 3) chords used conform to a hyper scale then perhaps it doesn't hurt too much if some of the other notes in these chords do not belong to a Hyper scale (i.e. some of the other notes make low strength melodic intervals).

If I use 10/9 instead of 9/8 in the scale above I get a Hyper scale but I lose the major chord on 3/2 (the V chord) if every note in the chord must belong to the scale.

The Root Notes (tonics) of Scales

Look at this scale...
1/1, 9/8, 5/4, 4/3, 3/2, 5/3, 15/8, 2/1

If I multiply each ratio by 24 I get...
24:27:30:32:36:40:45:48

These numbers separated by colons I call an IRS (an Integer Representation of a Scale which shows the proportions of all the frequencies in the scale). Similarly for chords I use the term IRC (Integer Representation of a Chord).

It seems to me that if a 1, 2, 4, 8 or 16 occurs in an IRS or or IRC then it is strongly rooted. These numbers are powers of 2 (2 to power of zero is 1). I think that higher powers of 2 such as 32 or 64 or 128 don't quite cut it. So the scale above is not strongly rooted. The lowest note does sound somewhat rooted but not *strongly rooted*. If I omit 9/8 and 15/8 I get this scale...

12:15:16:18:20:24

There is a 16 here and this note is the root note of the scale

33

even though it is not the lowest note. So this scale is strongly rooted. I could use the phrase "strong tonic" as well but I prefer "strongly rooted". So if you are playing a melody using only these six notes then the melody will sound resolved and satisfying if you finish (or *land*) on the 16.

I am naming these powers of 2 from 1 to 16 as P2s. In other words a 1, 2, 4, 8, or 16 could be called a P2. Higher powers of 2 such as 32, 64 or 128 are not P2s. Some scales may have more than one P2. If it does then the lowest P2 is the root note.

A good demonstration of this idea is the four-note 3:4:5:6 scale. If 3 is E then the four notes are E, A, C#, E. Play these notes in any order on any regular Western instrument and the second note (A) will clearly sound like the root note or tonic (most resolved sounding note) even though it is not the lowest note.

This power of 2 as a root note idea seems strange and counter intuitive to me. For a long time I thought that the root note of a chord or scale should always be the lowest note but the 3:4:5:6 scale above clearly disproves that idea.

For my taste there is something lacking in a chord or scale if it doesn't have a P2 in the IRC or IRS. I think that they are inferior to chords or scales that *have* a P2. At one point I considered that chords or scales with no P2 in the IRC or IRS should be illegal but I'm open to using them now.

Looking at 3:5:7:11 as a scale (there is no P2 here) there seems to be no point of rest. Play the notes in any order but you will never find a satisfying note to *land* on. In other words there is no note here that sounds *resolved or a point of rest*.

Chapter Six
Harmony and Chords

My formula for quantifying the strength value of a just *melodic* interval (two notes played one after the other) is $2/x + 2/y$. I think that the same formula applies to harmony intervals (two notes played simultaneously) as well but in a harmony context there is a dissonance factor (called beating) that needs to be acknowledged also.

Consider two notes with frequencies of 220Hz (waves per second) and 234.667Hz. These frequencies correspond to the just 16/15 interval. When you play these notes simultaneously an unpleasant sound can be heard which sounds like a wobble or a growl. If you have a piano or guitar nearby play two notes simultaneously that are only a semitone apart and you will clearly hear the unpleasant sound which is called *beating*. The frequency of the beats is the higher frequency minus the lower frequency, in this case 234.667Hz - 220Hz = 14.667Hz. So in this example there are 14.667 beats per second.

Beating isn't confined to narrow intervals. The 15/7 harmony interval is wider than an octave but beating can be heard between the 15 and the 7's first overtone (which is 14). The beating isn't as loud as it would be among two fundamentals (the first overtone is only half as loud as the fundamental) but it is definitely audible.

Periodicity in Harmony Intervals

As I said earlier, my formula for quantifying the strength values of melodic intervals was originally $1/x + 1/y$ (it's now $2/x + 2/y$). I assumed that this same formula ($1/x + 1/y$) should apply to the periodicity (*harmony*) aspect of a harmony interval (ignoring the beating aspect) as well. Putting $3/2$ in the formula I got $1/3 + 1/2 = 0.8333$. $5/3$ gave me 0.5333. $6/5$ gave me 0.3667. To my ear, any just harmony interval with a value of 0.5 or higher sounded high strength. Also any just interval with a value less than 0.5 sounded medium to low strength.

I described the following in the last chapter but it's worth repeating. At one point I decided that any pair of notes played simultaneously make a high strength interval if they sound stronger than either note played on it's own. Also any two notes played simultaneously are medium to low strength if they sound weaker than either note played on its own. I assumed that a single note on its own should have a strength value of 1. So theoretically any harmony interval, using the $1/x + 1/y$ formula, with a value less than 1 should sound weak but in practice this is not the case. $3/2$ and $5/3$ have periodicity values less than 1.0 using the $1/x + 1/y$ formula yet they both sound very strong. Because of this I guessed that maybe the formula should be doubled to get $2/x + 2y$ instead. Perhaps the result should be doubled because two notes are involved. I can't prove that $2/x + 2/y$ is the correct formula but I did some listening tests on it and it seems reasonable. Using the $2/x + 2/y$ formula, $3/2$ gives a result of 1.6667 and $5/3$ gives a result of 1.0667, both results are greater than 1 and both intervals sound very strong to my ears. Harmony intervals with a value less than 1.0 definitely sound medium or low strength to me.

Using the $2/x + 2/y$ formula I thought that any harmony interval with a value of 0.5 or higher should be acceptable and those with a value less than 0.5 should be rather weak and therefore avoided. However I like $11/7$, $10/7$ and $12/7$ which have values between 0.4 and 0.5 (values lower than 0.5) so I lowered the threshold from 0.5 to 0.4 (from $2/4$ to $2/5$).

Quantifying the Strength Values of Chords

I'm not 100% sure about this but I've done a few listening tests and it seems reasonable. Consider a six note major chord 2:3:4:5:6:8. I call these numbers the IRC of a chord (Integer Representation of a Chord). Add the inverse or reciprocal of each number to get: $0.5 + 0.333 + 0.25 + 0.2 + 0.167 + 0.125 = 1.575$. Now multiply 1.575 by 2 to get 3.15. If my method is right this is the overall strength value of the chord.

So to calculate the overall strength of any chord add the inverses of the numbers in the IRC and multiply this sum by 2.

Note that every interval in a given chord must (for me at least) be within 8.474 cents of a good (value greater than or equal to 0.4 using the $2/x + 2/y$ formula) just interval. See the list of good just harmony intervals two pages ahead. If a chord has duplicates (e.g. 2:3:4:3:4 has two 3s and two 4s) use them in the formula as well.

If the strength value of a chord is 0.4 or greater then the chord is, for me, acceptable.

If the strength value of a chord is below 0.4 then the chord is too weak for me and I won't use it.

Many chords contain intervals that are all good in themselves but the overall strength value is less than 0.4. I won't use these chords.

The Root Notes of Chords

Finding the root notes of chords is the same as for scales. If one or more P2s (1, 2, 4, 8 or 16) occurs in an IRC (Integer Representation of a Chord) then the lowest P2 is the root note of the chord. If a chord contains a P2 in its IRC then the chord is "strongly rooted".

Many chords do not contain a P2 (e.g. the 3:5:7:9 chord).

These chords are *not* strongly rooted. To me they sound a bit vague, restless and unresolved and I'm not overly fond of them. Strongly rooted chords are named according to their root note.

How to name 3:5:7:9? After reduction, there is one interval in the chord that contains a P2 and that is 3:9 which reduces to 1:3. 1 is a P2 so the chord perhaps should be named after it's lowest note. You could argue that 3:5:7:9 is *slightly* rooted (the 3 is the weak root) but I think that chords that aren't strongly rooted (no P2) are inferior to chords that are. 3:5:7 has no P2 anywhere even if you try to reduce 3:5, 3:7 and 5:7. I would name this 3:5:7 chord after its lowest note.

The 7:9:12 chord has no P2 but when you reduce 9:12 to 3:4 you get a P2 (in this case 4) so I would name the chord after its highest note (the 12 in 7:9:12).

For a while I wouldn't use chords that are not strongly rooted but now I think they are acceptable as long as they have an overall strength value >=0.4.

Lush Chords

Chords that have an overall strength (or periodicity) value >=0.75 and are strongly rooted (contain a 1, 2, 4, 8 or 16 in their IRC) I call *Lush Chords*. These are the very best chords for my taste.

Good Harmony Intervals

Here is a list of harmony intervals over a two octave range that have values greater than 0.4 using the $2/x + 2/y$ formula. The ratios on the left are just intervals, the numbers in the middle are the widths of the intervals in cents and the numbers on the right are the strength values using the $2/x + 2/y$ formula.

1/1 =	0.0	cents	4.00
10/9 =	182.404	cents	0.42
9/8 =	203.91	cents	0.47
8/7 =	231.174	cents	0.54
7/6 =	266.871	cents	0.62
6/5 =	315.641	cents	0.73
11/9 =	347.408	cents	0.40
5/4 =	386.314	cents	0.90
9/7 =	435.084	cents	0.51
4/3 =	498.045	cents	1.17
11/8 =	551.318	cents	0.43
7/5 =	582.512	cents	0.69
10/7 =	617.488	cents	0.49
3/2 =	701.955	cents	1.67
11/7 =	782.492	cents	0.47
8/5 =	813.686	cents	0.65

```
13/8  = 840.528  cents    0.40

 5/3  = 884.359  cents    1.07

12/7  = 933.129  cents    0.45

 7/4  = 968.826  cents    0.79

 9/5  = 1017.6   cents    0.62

11/6  = 1049.36  cents    0.52

13/7  = 1071.7   cents    0.44

 2/1  = 1200     cents    3.00

15/7  = 1319.44  cents    0.42

13/6  = 1338.57  cents    0.49

11/5  = 1365     cents    0.58

 9/4  = 1403.91  cents    0.72

16/7  = 1431.17  cents    0.41

 7/3  = 1466.87  cents    0.95

12/5  = 1515.64  cents    0.57

17/7  = 1536.13  cents    0.40

 5/2  = 1586.31  cents    1.40

13/5  = 1654.21  cents    0.55

 8/3  = 1698.04  cents    0.92

11/4  = 1751.32  cents    0.68
```

```
14/5 = 1782.51 cents    0.54

17/6 = 1803    cents     0.45

 3/1 = 1901.96 cents    2.67

19/6 = 1995.56 cents    0.44

16/5 = 2013.69 cents    0.53

13/4 = 2040.53 cents    0.65

10/3 = 2084.36 cents    0.87

17/5 = 2118.64 cents    0.52

 7/2 = 2168.83 cents    1.29

18/5 = 2217.6  cents    0.51

11/3 = 2249.36 cents    0.85

15/4 = 2288.27 cents    0.63

19/5 = 2311.2  cents    0.51

23/6 = 2326.32 cents    0.42

 4/1 = 2400    cents     2.50
```

When building chords not wider than two octaves every note, paired with every other note in the chord, must make an interval within 8.474 cents of any of the good harmony intervals listed above (for me at least). The five <u>underlined</u> intervals are an exception (see next page).

Using the $2/x + 2/y$ formula the cut off value here is 0.4 (i.e. if an interval has a value greater than 0.4 then it is good). The 13/8 interval has a value of 0.404 (greater than 0.4) and sounds good to my ears.

All of the good harmony intervals listed above (over a one octave range: between 1/1 and 2/1 inclusive) occur in Eagle 53 within 8.474 cents accuracy except for: 11/9, 11/8, 11/7, 11/6 and 13/8. Because these are all high prime limit (11 and 13, higher than 7) they don't pair well with many other notes and therefore I don't want them or miss them.

It seems to me that the 11/6, 13/7, 15/7, 13/6 and 11/5 intervals produce significant beating between the first overtone (2nd harmonics) of the lower note and the fundamental of the higher note. These intervals are underlined in the list above. I currently won't use these intervals in a chord. This applies to instruments whose tones produce a regular harmonic series. Using sine wave tones, which have no overtones, they should be acceptable.

Chapter Seven
The 2024/2019
Tempering Tolerance

In 12TET the perfect fourth (4/3) and perfect fifth (3/2) are both slightly out of tune by 2 cents yet they sound perfectly acceptable in a piece of music. There must be a tolerance within which an interval is acceptable.

I guessed that the tuning tolerance should look like n/d where n is a power of 2 and d is the same number minus 1. Why? Simply because it would look good (there is something about powers of 2). Like I said, it's only a guess that could be wrong.

I tried 128/127, 256/255 and 512/511 and the 256/255 seemed likely after a few listening tests. 256 is 2 to the power of 8. 256/255 expressed in cents is 6.7758 cents. I tested a few intervals that were out of tune by 6.7758 cents and although a very slight amount of "out of tuneness" could be detected they all sounded acceptable.

I used 256/255 as the maximum deviation from just for years but at one stage, a few years ago, I changed my mind. I have heard music in 19EDO where the major chords sounded sweet even though they contained a number of intervals that were out of tune by more than 256/255 or 6.7758 cents. I guessed that 1024/1019 might be a better tempering tolerance. Where did 2024/2019 come from?

256/255 is the same as 1024/1020 or 1024/(1024-4). A more relaxed threshold is 1024/1019 which is 1024/(1024-5) which is 8.474 cents. This is proportional to the shift I made from my 0.5 cut off point (using my formula for the strength of a harmony interval) to my 0.4 cut off point. Going from two quarters (0.5) to two fifths (0.4). This is more of a gut feeling than a mathematically provable idea.

Anyway, using either the stricter 256/255 or looser 1024/1019 as a tempering tolerance does not affect the main idea in this book which is the Eagle 53 tuning. All the notes in Eagle 53 (between 1/1 and 2/1) pair nicely melodically with both 1/1 and 2/1 within 256/255 (6.7758 cents) accuracy of just.

I think that the plus or minus 8.474 cents tempering tolerance applies to *all* intervals, weak or strong, using regular harmonic series tones, and also applies to *both* melody and harmony intervals.

Chapter Eight
Crow J.I.

A few years ago I worked out a just scale with eight notes (eight if you include 1/1 and 2/1) The scale is exotic as it contains a 7/6 (266.9 cents) and a 7/4 (968.8 cents) and is worth a mention here. The scale is...

1/1, 7/6, 5/4, 4/3, 3/2, 5/3, 7/4, 2/1

I call it Crow J.I. (J.I. stands for Just Intonation).

```
CROW J.I.
D       0.0 cents    1/1
E     266.9 cents    7/6
F     386.3 cents    5/4
G     498.0 cents    4/3
A     702.0 cents    3/2
B     884.4 cents    5/3
C     968.8 cents    7/4
D    1200.0 cents    2/1
```

The IRS looks like...

12:14:15:16:18:20:21:24

There is a P2 (16) in the IRS so the 16 (G) is the tonic or root note of the scale. The chords listed below, and any subset of a chord listed, should be good. The root note of each chord is often not the lowest note in the chord. If one or more P2s occur in a chord then the lowest P2 is the root note of the chord. If no P2 occurs then the chord is not strongly rooted.

```
D,A,D,F,A,C,D        2:3:4:5:6:7:8
D,G,B,D,E,G,A,D      3:4:5:6:7:8:9:12
```

```
D,G,B,D,E,G,B,D          3:4:5:6:7:8:10:12
D,F,A,C,D,F,A,C,D        4:5:6:7:8:10:12:14:16
D,E,G,A,D                6:7:8:9:12
D,E,G,B,D,E,G            6:7:8:10:12:14:16
D,G,A,D,A,D              6:8:9:12:18:24
D,B,D,F,A,D              6:10:12:15:18:24
D,B,D,F,B,D              6:10:12:15:20:24

E,C,E,C,E                2:3:4:6:8
E,G,A,D                  7:8:9:12
E,G,B,D,E,G              7:8:10:12:14:16
E,A,D,C                  7:9:12:21
E,D,E,C                  7:12:14:21

F,B,F,B,F                3:4:6:8:12
F,A,C,D,F,A,C,D          5:6:7:8:10:12:14:16
F,A,D,F,A,C,D,F          5:6:8:10:12:14:16:20
G,D,G,B,D,E,G            2:3:4:5:6:7:8
G,B,D,E,G,A,D            4:5:6:7:8:9:12
G,B,D,E,G,B,D,E,G        4:5:6:7:8:10:12:14:16
G,B,D,A,D,F              4:5:6:9:12:15
G,B,D,B,D,F              4:5:6:10:12:15
G,A,D,A,D                8:9:12:18:24

A,D,F,A,C,D,F,A          3:4:5:6:7:8:10:12
A,C,D,F,A,C,D            6:7:8:10:12:14:16

B,F,B,F,B                2:3:4:6:8
B,D,E,G,A,D              5:6:7:8:9:12
B,D,E,G,B,D,E,G          5:6:7:8:10:12:14:16
B,D,G,B,D,E,G,A          5:6:8:10:12:14:16:18
B,D,G,B,D,E,G,B          5:6:8:10:12:14:16:20
B,D,A,D,F,A              5:6:9:12:15:18
B,D,B,D,F,A              5:6:10:12:15:18
B,D,B,D,F,B              5:6:10:12:15:20

C,E,C,E,C                3:4:6:8:12
C,D,F,A,C,D              7:8:10:12:14:16
```

Chapter Nine
Eagle 53: My Ultimate Musical Tuning

When I began my research in 1995 I wanted to discover one single *ultimate* or best tuning (or scale). In 2010 my ultimate tuning was Blue Temperament. Later, in 2012, it was Raven Temperament. As of 22nd June, 2016 my ultimate tuning is Eagle 53 and currently I don't think I could improve on it.

This chapter describes how I worked it out. I am choosing to use exactly twelve notes per octave partly because it is easy to implement on a guitar or regular keyboard. If I add just one extra note beyond the twelve per octave that I have here then on a small fretted stringed instrument (e.g. ukulele or mandolin) some frets would be too close to each other for comfortable playing.

When I worked out Eagle JI (described below) I used melody intervals with values higher than 0.25 (I now use a cut off of 0.2) but using either list won't affect the resulting tuning. I also used a stricter tempering tolerance of 6.7758 cents (256/255) instead of my current 8.474 cents (2024/2019) tolerance but again, using either one won't affect the resulting tuning. Both the 0.25 cut off point and the 6.7758 cents tempering tolerance (which I use below) are stricter than what I use now (0.2 and 8.474 cents) but either way the resulting tuning will be the same.

Here we go: below is a list of just melodic intervals whose strength values are greater than 0.25 using the $2/x + 2/y$ formula over a one octave range. I used this list as a *map* when working out Eagle J.I. (J.I. is short for Just Intonation). Intervals with a value greater than 1.0 are high strength and intervals with a value between 0.25 and 0.999 are medium strength intervals. The strength values are shown in the middle column. The numbers on the right are the widths of the intervals in cents.

1/1	4	0.0000
16/15	0.2583	111.7313
15/14	0.2762	119.4428
14/13	0.2967	128.2982
13/12	0.3205	138.5727
12/11	0.3485	150.6371
11/10	0.3818	165.0042
10/9	0.4222	182.4037
9/8	0.4722	203.9100
17/15	0.2510	216.6867
8/7	0.5357	231.1741
15/13	0.2872	247.7411
7/6	0.6190	266.8709
13/11	0.3357	289.2097
6/5	0.7333	315.6413
17/14	0.2605	336.1295
11/9	0.4040	347.4079
16/13	0.2788	359.4723
5/4	0.9000	386.3137
14/11	0.3247	417.5080
9/7	0.5079	435.0841
13/10	0.3538	454.2140
17/13	0.2715	464.4278
4/3	1.1667	498.0450
15/11	0.3152	536.9508
11/8	0.4318	551.3179
18/13	0.2650	563.3823
7/5	0.6857	582.5122
17/12	0.2843	603.0004
10/7	0.4857	617.4878
13/9	0.3761	636.6177
16/11	0.3068	648.6821
19/13	0.2591	656.9854
3/2	1.6667	701.9550
20/13	0.2538	745.7861
17/11	0.2995	753.6375
14/9	0.3651	764.9159
11/7	0.4675	782.4920
19/12	0.2719	795.5580

8/5	0.6500	813.6863
13/8	0.4038	840.5277
18/11	0.2929	852.5921
5/3	1.0667	884.3587
17/10	0.3176	918.6417
12/7	0.4524	933.1291
19/11	0.2871	946.1951
7/4	0.7857	968.8259
16/9	0.3472	996.0900
9/5	0.6222	1017.5963
20/11	0.2818	1034.9958
11/6	0.5152	1049.3629
13/7	0.4396	1071.7018
15/8	0.3833	1088.2687
17/9	0.3399	1101.0454
19/10	0.3053	1111.1993
21/11	0.2771	1119.4630
23/12	0.2536	1126.3193
2/1	3	1200.0000

First of all, like most tunings, I start with two notes (1/1 and 2/1, an octave apart) and then add some notes in between. The tuning will be *octave repeating* (meaning that the notes in any given octave range will have frequencies exactly double that of the notes in the octave just below it and the notes will have frequencies exactly half of those in the octave just above it).

I think that the melodic aspect of a tuning is more important than the harmony aspect. Having a lot of good chords available is not much good if you can't play a decent melody. As I said above I use the list of high strength and medium strength melodic intervals above as a *map* when I am working out a tuning.

At one point I wanted every note in the new tuning, when paired with every other note (over a one octave range) to make a good melodic interval within 6.7758 cents accuracy of any interval in the list above. If I use the obvious notes (1/1, 6/5, 4/3, 3/2, 5/3 and 2/1) and add seven more notes among them this can't be done, a few low strength melodic intervals will be inevitable.

I consider the tonics 1/1 and 2/1 to be more important than the notes in between and what *can* be done is to find eleven notes between 1/1 and 2/1 that make high or medium strength intervals when paired melodically with *both* 1/1 *and* 2/1. Low strength intervals may occur elsewhere in the tuning but never in an interval that contains either the 1/1 or 2/1 and another note in between.

Starting with 1/1 and 2/1, I add 4/3 and 3/2 to the tuning. Both 4/3 and 3/2 are high strength melodically when paired with both 1/1 and 2/1. I now have...

1/1, __, __, __, __, 4/3, __, 3/2, __, __, __, __, 2/1

Next I add 5/3 because it is high strength melodically when paired with 1/1 and is medium strength paired with 2/1.

Next I add 6/5 because it is high strength melodically when paired with 2/1 and is also good (medium strength) when paired with 1/1. I now have...

1/1, __, __, 6/5, __, 4/3, __, 3/2, __, 5/3, __, __, 2/1

Between 6/5 and 4/3 I have these possibilities...

6/5	0.7333	315.6413
17/14	0.2605	336.1295
11/9	0.4040	347.4079
16/13	0.2788	359.4723
5/4	0.9000	386.3137
14/11	0.3247	417.5080
9/7	0.5079	435.0841
13/10	0.3538	454.2140
17/13	0.2715	464.4278
4/3	1.1667	498.0450

5/4 is the obvious choice as it is good melodically when paired with both 1/1 and 2/1 and is stronger than 9/7. So 5/4 is in.

Between 4/3 and 3/2 I have these possibilities...

```
  4/3    1.1667    498.0450
15/11    0.3152    536.9508
 11/8    0.4318    551.3179
18/13    0.2650    563.3823
  7/5    0.6857    582.5122
17/12    0.2843    603.0004
 10/7    0.4857    617.4878
 13/9    0.3761    636.6177
16/11    0.3068    648.6821
19/13    0.2591    656.9854
  3/2    1.6667    701.9550
```

   The likeliest candidates here are 7/5 and 10/7. I consider 1/1 to be more resolved (and therefore more important) than 2/1 and 7/5 goes better with 1/1 than 10/7 so I'm choosing 7/5.

Between 3/2 and 5/3 I have these possibilities...

```
  3/2    1.6667    701.9550
20/13    0.2538    745.7861
17/11    0.2995    753.6375
 14/9    0.3651    764.9159
 11/7    0.4675    782.4920
19/12    0.2719    795.5580
  8/5    0.6500    813.6863
 13/8    0.4038    840.5277
18/11    0.2929    852.5921
  5/3    1.0667    884.3587
```

8/5 is the obvious choice here so 8/5 is in.

I now have...

   1/1, __, __, 6/5, 5/4, 4/3, 7/5, 3/2, 8/5, 5/3, __, __, 2/1.

   At this point I'm changing tactics because I want a major chord on 1/1 and 4/3 and 3/2. This is called a I, IV, V chord progression: the root notes of the three major chords correspond to 6:8:9 (multiply 1/1 and 4/3 and 3/2 by 6 to get 6:8:9). If the tonic is E, I want the E major, A major and B major chords available. Using the 9 notes listed above, if 1/1 is E, the E major and A major chords are available but not the B major. If I add 9/8 and 15/8 to the scale then the B major chord becomes available (i.e. the I, IV and V chords are now available). I think that the I, IV, V chord progressions (in various combinations) are the most common progressions in Western music. So 9/8 and 15/8 are in. 9/8 and 15/8 are both good melodically when paired with 1/1 and 2/1. I now have...

1/1, __, 9/8, 6/5, 5/4, 4/3, 7/5, 3/2, 8/5, 5/3, __, 15/8, 2/1.

Between 1/1 and 9/8 I have these possibilities...

1/1	4	0.0000
16/15	0.2583	111.7313
15/14	0.2762	119.4428
14/13	0.2967	128.2982
13/12	0.3205	138.5727
12/11	0.3485	150.6371
11/10	0.3818	165.0042
10/9	0.4222	182.4037
9/8	0.4722	203.9100

10/9 is too close to 9/8 to be implemented on a fretted instrument (the frets would be too close together for comfortable playing). 11/10, 12/11, 13/12 and 14/13 contain primes 11 or 13 and therefore will not pair nicely with the other notes chosen so far. 15/14 does not pair well with 2/1 (it makes 28/15, which is not in the list of good intervals). 16/15 is good, 2/1 over 16/15 gives 15/8, a medium strength melodic interval. So I'm choosing 16/15.

Between 5/3 and 15/8 I have these possibilities...

5/3	1.0667	884.3587
17/10	0.3176	918.6417
12/7	0.4524	933.1291
19/11	0.2871	946.1951
7/4	0.7857	968.8259
16/9	0.3472	996.0900
9/5	0.6222	1017.5963
20/11	0.2818	1034.9958
11/6	0.5152	1049.3629
13/7	0.4396	1071.7018
15/8	0.3833	1088.2687

The likely candidates here are 12/7, 7/4, 16/9, 9/5 and 11/6. 12/7 is too close to 5/3 for small fretted instruments. 7/4 is okay but being a 7 limit note will not pair well with many other notes. 16/9 is okay too but it is not as strong as 9/5. 11/6 has prime 11 and will not pair well with many other notes. Using 9/5 introduces another major chord on the 6/5 note so I'm choosing 9/5 which also pairs nicely with 2/1. I have often reconsidered 16/9 but I definitely want a major chord (2:3:4:5:6:8) on 6/5 so I'm sticking with 9/5. If 1/1 is E then using 9/5 means that major chords are available on C, F and G (another I, IV, V group). I now have a 12 note per octave just scale which I call Eagle J.I....

1/1, 16/15, 9/8, 6/5, 5/4, 4/3, 7/5, 3/2, 8/5, 5/3, 9/5, 15/8, 2/1.

As I said earlier, there is no room for additional notes as these would not be suitable for small fretted instruments (i.e. the distances between some frets would be too small for comfortable playing). This just tuning is not new. Back in the 90s I read somewhere that it is called something like "Just Major with 7 limit tritone" and I'm not sure who worked it out first, possibly it was a man called Robert Rich.

There is no strong chord on the 15/8 so the scale needs to be tempered (adjusted slightly). I raised the second note, 16/15, by 1.6 cents (from 111.7c to 113.3c) so that it could function as a 15/14 as well (within 6.7758 cents accuracy). I also raised the seventh note, 7/5, by 1.6 cents (from 582.5c to 584.1c) so that a minor chord could be played on the twelfth note (15/8) where all of the intervals in the chord are within 6.7758 cents of just.

I don't think that this is the best possible tempering of the Eagle J.I.. In May or June of 2016 I posted this just scale on one of the Facebook tuning groups and (as I said in the introduction) a prominent member of the group, Paul Erlich, suggested "tempering out the marvel comma, 225/224". I didn't fully understand what this means but another member of the group, Jake Freivald, also thought of tempering out 225/224 and thought that *quantising* the scale to an EDO that tempers out 225/224 might be good.

As mentioned in the chapter on other alternative tunings, EDO stands for Equal Division of the Octave. Jake proposed three EDOs that temper out 225/224 and these were 41EDO, 53EDO and 72EDO. Note that only 12 notes (all within +/- 6.7758 cents of the 12 notes in Eagle JI) in each EDO are used and the others are discarded. In the end (on 22nd June, 2016) I chose the 12 note subset of 53EDO, as my favourite, or ultimate, tuning. This tuning is the most accurate of the three EDOs suggested by Jake. I'm calling it Eagle 53, or just Eagle. Thanks to Paul and Jake for their input towards the finding of Eagle 53.

As I said in the introduction Eagle 53 may not be new. It is the same as a 53EDO version of both Euler's Genus Diatonico-chromaticum scale and Ellis' Duodene scale, both of which are identical to Eagle JI except that they used 45/32 (590.2c) instead of my 7/5 (582.5c). I do not know if the exact 12 notes (no subsets or supersets) of Eagle 53 have ever been documented before I came up with it in 2016.

Here is a quote from a post by Jake on the Xenharmonic2 tuning group on Facebook which describes how we got from Eagle JI to Eagle 53. Words in {square brackets} are mine.

Jake   <<<

Here's how it looked to me. The bottom line is that there were some practical considerations to be met, and then John could get back to making music. The more time spent on theory, the less helpful my role would be.

Here's the long version:

I spoke to John a lot about his specific criteria, and he didn't seem worried at all about 11- or 13-limit intervals. He's mostly a pragmatic guy, an empiricist above all, but with a little bit of "numerology" about him (e.g., when I read his first book, his decision to go with a 256/255 error boundary seemed to be related as much to his love of powers of two as anything else). He's not a deeply theoretical guy, though; he didn't understand comma tempering, which was the main way I thought I could help him.

And that was the real point: I just wanted to help John hit some relatively simple goals. This wasn't a be-all-end-all tuning quest -- it was an engineering problem, not a mathematical one, if you get my meaning.

I saw John starting to temper Eagle JI computationally, tweaking a note here or there to see what popped up, and thought I could help him find a solution by tempering out a comma or two. I analyzed Eagle JI I realized that it would hit all of John's criteria if I tempered out Marvel. Looking back on the thread we were in, I saw that Paul had already suggested that. So Marvel it was to be.

Now, there are a variety of ways to temper out a comma. I could have put Eagle JI into Scala and had it do the math for me. But I personally find it easier, given the software that I have to write music, to temper to an EDO.

It's important to note (as much as any of this is important) tempering to an EDO is important for ME personally, not John. For instance, I wrote some stuff in Starling a while back, and it was a pain in the neck to implement. Over the course of several years, I ended up having all kinds of directories filled with all kinds of different MOS temperaments tuned to their POTE optimums, and it was a pain using them. It became much easier to just pick a suitable EDO and use it. (This, by the way, answers a question I asked about 8 years ago when I was still a newb on the old Tuning list: Why bother with EDOs when computers can tune to any value? Answer: They get rid of a lot of setup issues and get you to the point of making music faster.) If I were going to write something new in Starling I would probably just use a 31-EDO subset because I already have that set up for Mus2. (Unless, of course, I had a reason not to use 31 -- say, I want to temper out 364/363 as well, so I might use 46 instead. I have that set up in Mus2, too. But I'd still use an EDO.)

ANYWAY... :) I picked three EDOs [these were 41EDO, 53EDO and 72EDO] that tempered out the magic comma and met John's criteria. I shipped the resulting scales off to John, and he picked one [53EDO]. Task complete, easy-peasy.

I get the impression (he'll correct me if I'm wrong) that he really liked the idea of the fifths being so close to JI [I do]. Distortion guitar will do that to a person. :)

Yes, of course there are additional commas tempered out by 53 EDO, and there are aspects of the specific tuning that may be suboptimal for some people's criteria. Those are probably worth exploring for some people. But those are all, it seems to me, "accidental" with respect to John's criteria -- cool, maybe, but not really an issue -- and not really worth bothering John about.

The stuff to bother John about (again, it seems to me, I hope I'm not putting words in his mouth too much) are things like, "Why those formulas? Why prioritize melodic vs. harmonic? What about this other possible criterion for your definition of "good interval"?" and so on, because those are the things that he actually thinks about and cares about and has done deep empirical research on.

In my opinion, of course. >>> Jake

Here is a short overview of Eagle 53...

```
 1/1       0.0 cents           just
16/15   113.2075c   sharp of just by 1.5 cents
 9/8    203.7736c    flat of just by 0.1 cents
 6/5    316.9811c   sharp of just by 1.3 cents
 5/4    384.9057c    flat of just by 1.4 cents
 4/3    498.1132c   sharp of just by 0.1 cents
 7/5    588.6792c   sharp of just by 6.2 cents
 3/2    701.8868c    flat of just by 0.1 cents
 8/5    815.0943c   sharp of just by 1.4 cents
 5/3    883.0189c    flat of just by 1.3 cents
 9/5   1018.8679c   sharp of just by 1.3 cents
15/8   1086.7925c    flat of just by 1.5 cents
 2/1   1200.0c            just
```

Here are some chords that occur in Eagle 53.

```
 1/1   2:3:4:5:6:8
16/15  2:3:4:5:6:8  and  2:3:4:5:7*
 9/8   4:5:8:10:16
 6/5   2:3:4:5:6:8
 5/4   2:3:4:6:8
 4/3   2:3:4:5:6:8
 7/5   7:10:14:20*  (20/7 ≈ 17/6)
 3/2   2:3:4:5:6:8
 8/5   2:3:4:5:6:8  and  2:3:4:5:7*
 5/3   2:3:4:6:8
 9/5   4:5:8:10:16
15/8   2:3:4:6:8
```

The last time I checked it looked like all of the intervals in all of these chords (except the chords marked with a *) are within 1.4 cents of just.

A regular Major chord on a guitar is 2:3:4:5:6:8
A regular Minor chord on a guitar is 10:15:20:24:30:40

If the tonic, 1/1, is E then on a guitar fretted and tuned to Eagle 53 the following chords (except the one on A#, the tritone) are within 1.4 cents of just... Regular major and minor chords are listed below.

E   major and minor
F   major
F# 4:5:8:10
G   major
G# minor
A   major and minor
A# 7:10:14:20 (20/7≈17/6)
B   major and minor
C   major
C# minor
D   2:4:5:8 and 6:10:12:15
D# minor

I said that with Eagle 53 stringed and fretted instruments there is no room for more frets without compromising playability. With an *equal* tuning (the interval between any two adjacent notes is always the same) more frets *could* be used, at least on larger instruments. I'm thinking about 19EDO, 19 frets per octave. 19EDO is my favorite EDO where *every* note (not a subset as in Eagle 53) has a corresponding fret on a guitar. Melodically you can't play a sour note if you avoid one-step intervals (63 cents). Major and Minor chords are all within 7.3 cents accuracy in 19EDO. Check out my treatise on 19EDO at...

www.johnsmusic7.com/19EDO.pdf

Eagle 53 is not an equal tuning and adding an extra note (and corresponding frets) would make some chords (in particular some barre chords) harder or impossible to play on smaller stringed and fretted instruments. So I'm sticking with the 12 notes per octave that I have here.

Chapter Ten
Eagle 53 Scales

I could name the notes in Eagle numerically. For example 1/1 is note 1, 16/15 is note 2, 9/8 is note 3, etc. There are some low strength melodic intervals in Eagle 53. If 1/1 is E these are...

Notes 3 and 10 (679 cents) F# and C#
Notes 4 and 5 (68 cents) G and G#
Notes 7 and 14 (725 cents) A# and F
Notes 9 and 10 (68 cents) C and C#
Notes 11 and 12 (68 cents) D and D#
Notes 11 and 18 (679 cents) D and A

So when playing a melody (or chord progression) one or the other of each pair of notes (or chords whose root notes correspond to the notes above) listed above could be used but not both (for me at least).

Six of the twelve notes (per octave) in Eagle have a good fourth (4/3) and fifth (3/2) above them. These six notes are: note 1 (1/1), note 4 (6/5), note 5 (4/3), note 8 (3/2), note 9 (8/5) and note 12 (15/8). Up until recently (perhaps late 2019 or early 2020) I wanted all my scales to have both 4/3 and 3/2 in them. Now I don't care as long as all the notes pair nicely with each other.

As I said in chapter five, any scale, that contains only high or medium strength (no low strength) melodic intervals (over a one octave range and within 8.474 cents of just) is a Hyper Scale. I have identified 30 seven notes per octave hyper scales in Eagle 53. There are 12 hyper scales on note 1, 3 hyper scales on note 4, 3 hyper scales on note 5 and 12 hyper scales on note 8. Also, in all of these 30 scales you never get 3 or more notes bunched up close together (i.e. there are never more than two adjacent notes used, so C, C#,D is illegal but C, C#, D# is allowed).

I have also added one extra hyper scale on 8/5 (C) because I wanted at least one scale where the lowest note is on 8/5 (C). This scale *does* have three notes bunched up close together but it was the strongest scale available on 8/5.

Below are the 31 scales. In each listing the first line is the name of the scale followed by the note number the scale begins on (e.g. Melodic Minor 4 has its root note on note 4). The second line shows the note number of each note in the scale. The third line shows the cent values of the distances of each note from the first note in the scale which is either note 1, 4, 5, 8 or 9. The fourth line shows the strong just notes which are within 8.474 cents of the actual notes listed and the fifth line shows the note names if note 1 corresponds to the key of E.

None of these 31 scales illustrated below are strongly rooted (no P2 in the IRS). The tonic or root note is not always the lowest note. I suggest playing all eight notes in a chosen scale back and forth in sequence. Any note that sounds somewhat resolved could be used as the tonic or root note of the scale. Some scales may have more than one note that sounds resolved.

Melodic Major 1

1	3	5	6	8	9	11	13
0	204	385	498	702	815	1019	1200
1/1	9/8	5/4	4/3	3/2	8/5	9/5	2/1
E	F#	G#	A	B	C	D	E

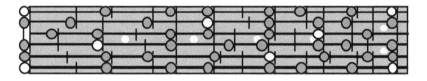

Arabian 1

1	2	5	6	8	9	12	13
0	113	385	498	702	815	1087	1200
1/1	16/15	5/4	4/3	3/2	8/5	15/8	2/1
E	F	G#	A	B	C	D#	E

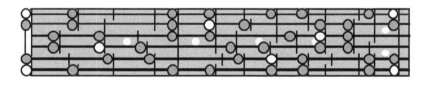

Neapolitan Major 1

1	2	4	6	8	10	12	13
0	113	317	498	702	883	1087	1200
1/1	16/15	6/5	4/3	3/2	5/3	15/8	2/1
E	F	G	A	B	C#	D#	E

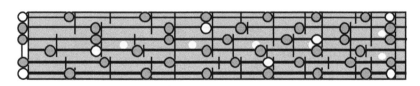

Phrygian 1

1	2	4	6	8	9	11	13
0	113	317	498	702	815	1019	1200
1/1	16/15	6/5	4/3	3/2	8/5	9/5	2/1
E	F	G	A	B	C	D	E

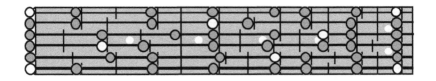

Natural Minor 1

1	3	4	6	8	9	11	13
0	204	317	498	702	815	1019	1200
1/1	9/8	6/5	4/3	3/2	8/5	9/5	2/1
E	F#	G	A	B	C	D	E

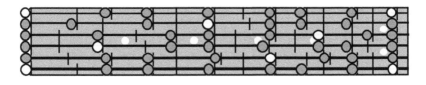

Gondolin 1

1	2	5	6	8	10	12	13
0	113	385	498	702	883	1087	1200
1/1	16/15	5/4	4/3	3/2	5/3	15/8	2/1
E	F	G#	A	B	C#	D#	E

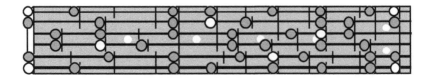

Neapolitan Minor 1

1	2	4	6	8	9	12	13
0	113	317	498	702	815	1087	1200
1/1	16/15	6/5	4/3	3/2	8/5	15/8	2/1
E	F	G	A	B	C	D#	E

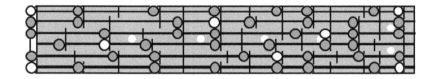

Harmonic Major 1

1	3	5	6	8	9	12	13
0	204	385	498	702	815	1087	1200
1/1	9/8	5/4	4/3	3/2	8/5	15/8	2/1
E	F#	G#	A	B	C	D#	E

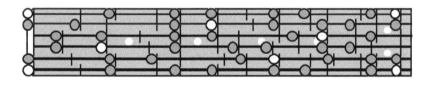

Numenor 1

1	2	5	6	8	9	11	13
0	113	385	498	702	815	1019	1200
1/1	16/15	5/4	4/3	3/2	8/5	9/5	2/1
E	F	G#	A	B	C	D	E

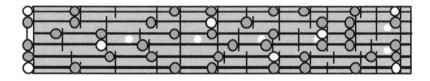

Lorien 1

1	2	5	6	8	10	11	13
0	113	385	498	702	883	1019	1200
1/1	16/15	5/4	4/3	3/2	5/3	9/5	2/1
E	F	G#	A	B	C#	D	E

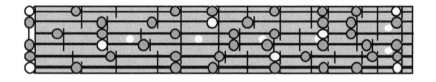

Harmonic Minor 1

1	3	4	6	8	9	12	13
0	204	317	498	702	815	1087	1200
1/1	9/8	6/5	4/3	3/2	8/5	15/8	2/1
E	F#	G	A	B	C	D#	E

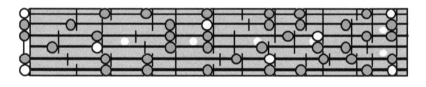

Rivendell 1

1	2	4	6	8	10	11	13
0	113	317	498	702	883	1019	1200
1/1	16/15	6/5	4/3	3/2	5/3	9/5	2/1
E	F	G	A	B	C#	D	E

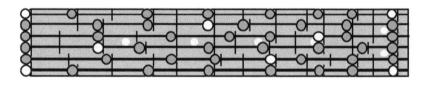

Major 4

4	6	8	9	11	13	15	16
0	181	385	498	702	883	1087	1200
1/1	10/9	5/4	4/3	3/2	5/3	15/8	2/1
G	A	B	C	D	E	F#	G

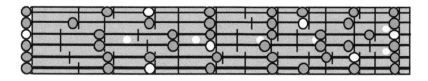

Mixolydian 4

4	6	8	9	11	13	14	16
0	181	385	498	702	883	996	1200
1/1	10/9	5/4	4/3	3/2	5/3	16/9	2/1
G	A	B	C	D	E	F	G

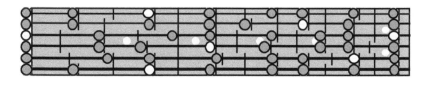

Melodic Minor 4

4	6	7	9	11	13	15	16
0	181	272	498	702	883	1087	1200
1/1	10/9	7/6	4/3	3/2	5/3	15/8	2/1
G	A	A#	C	D	E	F#	G

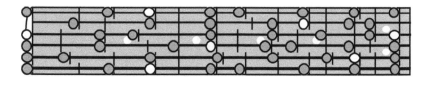

Phrygian 5

5	6	8	10	12	13	15	17
0	113	317	498	702	815	1019	1200
1/1	16/15	6/5	4/3	3/2	8/5	9/5	2/1
G#	A	B	C#	D#	E	F#	G#

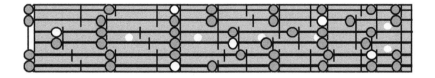

Natural Minor 5

5	7	8	10	12	13	15	17
0	204	317	498	702	815	1019	1200
1/1	9/8	6/5	4/3	3/2	8/5	9/5	2/1
G#	A#	B	C#	D#	E	F#	G#

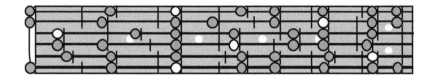

Rivendell 5

5	6	8	10	12	14	15	17
0	113	317	498	702	928	1019	1200
1/1	16/15	6/5	4/3	3/2	12/7	9/5	2/1
G#	A	B	C#	D#	F	F#	G#

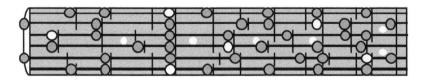

Melodic Major 8

8	10	12	13	15	16	18	20
0	181	385	498	702	815	996	1200
1/1	10/9	5/4	4/3	3/2	8/5	16/9	2/1
B	C#	D#	E	F#	G	A	B

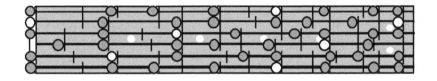

Arabian 8

8	9	12	13	15	16	19	20
0	113	385	498	702	815	1087	1200
1/1	16/15	5/4	4/3	3/2	8/5	15/8	2/1
B	C	D#	E	F#	G	A#	B

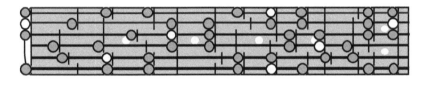

Neapolitan Major 8

8	9	11	13	15	17	19	20
0	113	317	498	702	883	1087	1200
1/1	16/15	6/5	4/3	3/2	5/3	15/8	2/1
B	C	D	E	F#	G#	A#	B

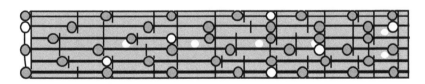

Major 8

8	10	12	13	15	17	19	20
0	181	385	498	702	883	1087	1200
1/1	10/9	5/4	4/3	3/2	5/3	15/8	2/1
B	C#	D#	E	F#	G#	A#	B

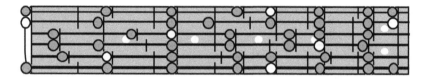

Mixolydian 8

8	10	12	13	15	17	18	20
0	181	385	498	702	883	996	1200
1/1	10/9	5/4	4/3	3/2	5/3	16/9	2/1
B	C#	D#	E	F#	G#	A	B

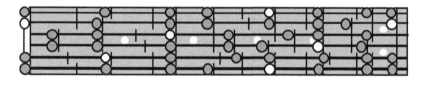

Gondolin 8

8	9	12	13	15	17	19	20
0	113	385	498	702	883	1087	1200
1/1	16/15	5/4	4/3	3/2	5/3	15/8	2/1
B	C	D#	E	F#	G#	A#	B

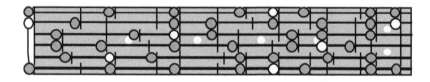

Neapolitan Minor 8

8	9	11	13	15	16	19	20
0	113	317	498	702	815	1087	1200
1/1	16/1	6/5	4/3	3/2	8/	15/8	2/1
B	C	D	E	F#	G	A#	B

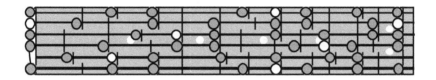

Harmonic Major 8

8	10	12	13	15	16	19	20
0	181	385	498	702	815	1087	1200
1/1	10/9	5/4	4/3	3/2	8/5	15/8	2/1
B	C#	D#	E	F#	G	A#	B

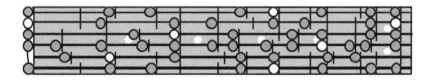

Numenor 8

8	9	12	13	15	16	18	20
0	113	385	498	702	815	996	1200
1/1	16/15	5/4	4/3	3/2	8/5	16/9	2/1
B	C	D#	E	F#	G	A	B

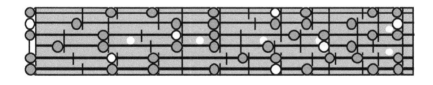

Lorien 8

8	9	12	13	15	17	18	20
0	113	385	498	702	883	996	1200
1/1	16/15	5/4	4/3	3/2	5/3	16/9	2/1
B	C	D#	E	F#	G#	A	B

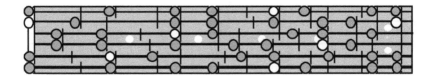

Harmonic Minor 8

8	10	11	13	15	16	19	20
0	181	317	498	702	815	1087	1200
1/1	10/9	6/5	4/3	3/2	8/5	15/8	2/1
B	C#	D	E	F#	G	A#	B

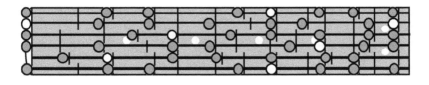

Melodic Minor 8

8	10	11	13	15	17	19	20
0	181	317	498	702	883	1087	1200
1/1	10/9	6/5	4/3	3/2	5/3	15/8	2/1
B	C#	D	E	F#	G#	A#	B

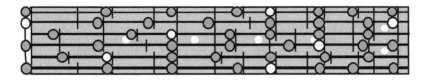

The Crow Scale on 9

9	12	13	14	16	18	19	21
0	272	385	498	702	883	974	1200
1/1	7/6	5/4	4/3	3/2	5/3	7/4	2/1
C	D#	E	F	G	A	A#	C

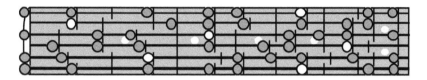

The Melodic Minor 4 and Rivendell 5 scales are a bit exotic as they contain a 7/6 (272 cents) and a 12/7 (928 cents) respectively.

There is a major (ish) scale on notes 4 and 8 which looks like:

$$1/1, \quad 10/9, \quad 5/4, \quad 4/3, \quad 3/2, \quad 5/3, \quad 15/8, \quad 2/1$$

but you won't get a major chord on 3/2 (the V chord). If there was a 9/8 instead of the 10/9 then the major chord on 3/2 (the V chord) would be available but this would not be a hyper scale (5/3 over 9/8 is 40/27 which is 680 cents, a low strength melodic interval which is for me illegal.

I want to have at least one scale that allows major chords on 1/1, 4/3 and 3/2. This scale looks like...

$$1/1, \quad 9/8, \quad 5/4, \quad 4/3, \quad 3/2, \quad 5/3, \quad 15/8, \quad 2/1$$

and as I said in chapter five I call it Major 145 (pronounced Major-one-four-five) because it contains the I, IV and V chords. Luckily this scale occurs on note 1(E) and note 9 (C) of Eagle 53 and therefore the I, IV and V chords are available using either notes 1 (E) or 9 (C) as the lowest note. Major 145 in Eagle 53 is *not* a hyper scale (again, 5/3 over 9/8 = 40/27, a low strength melodic interval). In 12TET it turns out that the Major 145 scale is *very* close to being a hyper scale, perhaps close enough if a tolerance of 2 cents greater than 8.474 cents is allowed, see chapter five.

I wrote about strongly rooted scales in chapter 5, scales that contain a P2 (1, 2, 4, 8 or 16) in the IRS. Look at the Major 145 scale...

1/1 9/8 5/4 4/3 3/2 5/3 15/8 2/1

Multiply each ratio by the lowest common multiple of the denominators (right hand sides), in this case 24, to get...

24:27:30:32:36:40:45:48

There is no P2 here so the scale is not strongly rooted (or has no strong tonic). 32 is a power of 2 but it is too weak I think, 16 is as far I go.

I worked out all the scales that are both hyper *and* strongly rooted (contain a P2 in the IRS) over a one octave range. Most of these are listed below (I omitted one or two that were weak or had three notes bunched up close together).

Note that any scale could be viewed as a chord progression as well if the root notes of each chord occur in the scale chosen. Here are the scales/ chord groups...

Strongly Rooted Scales/Chord Groups
Letters in [square brackets] indicate the root note or chord.

```
E
B, [E], G#, B   3:4:5:6
[E], G#, B, E   4:5:6:8
G#, B, [E], F#, G#   5:6:8:9:10
B, [E], F#, G#, B   6:8:9:10:12
[E], F#, G#, B, D#, E   8:9:10:12:15:16
F#, G#, B, D#, [E], F#   9:10:12:15:16:18
B, D#, [E], F#, G#, B   12:15:16:18:20:24


F
C, [F], A, C   3:4:5:6
[F], A, C, D#, F   4:5:6:7:8
A, C, D#, [F], G, A   5:6:7:8:9:10
C, D#, [F], G, A, C   6:7:8:9:10:12
D#, [F], G, A, C, D#   7:8:9:10:12:14
[F], G, A, C, D#, E, F   8:9:10:12:14:15:16
G, A, C, D#, E, [F], G   9:10:12:14:15:16:18
A, C, D#, E, [F], G, A   10:12:14:15:16:18:20
C, D#, E, [F], G, A, A#, C   12:14:15:16:18:20:21:24
D#, E, [F], G, A, A#, C, D   14:15:16:18:20:21:24:27
D#, E, [F], G, A, A#, C, D#   14:15:16:18:20:21:24:28
D#, E, [F], G, A, A#, C#, D   14:15:16:18:20:21:25:27
D#, E, [F], G, A, A#, C#, D#   14:15:16:18:20:21:25:28
E, [F], G, A, A#, C, D#   15:16:18:20:21:24:28
[F], G, A, A#, C,   16:18:20:21:24


F#
A#, [F#], A#   5:8:10


G
D, [G], B, D   3:4:5:6
[G], B, D, G   4:5:6:8
B, D, [G], B   5:6:8:10
[G], B, D, F#, G   8:10:12:15:16
B, D, F#, [G], B   10:12:15:16:20
D, F#, [G], B, D   12:15:16:20:24
```

```
G#
D#, [G#], A#, D#   6:8:9:12
[G#], A#, D#,G#   8:9:12:16
D#, [G#], A, A#, D#   12:16:17:18:24


A
E, [A], C#, E   3:4:5:6
[A], C#, E, A   4:5:6:8
C#, E, [A], B, C#   5:6:8:9:10
E, [A], B, C#, E   6:8:9:10:12
[A], B, C#, E, G#, A   8:9:10:12:15:16
B, C#, E, G#, [A], B   9:10:12:15:16:18
C#, E, G#, [A], B, C#   10:12:15:16:18:20
E, G#, [A], B, C#, E   12:15:16:18:20:24
G#, [A], B, C#, E, G#   15:16:18:20:24:30


B
F#, [B], D#, F#   3:4:5:6
[B], D#, F#, B   4:5:6:8
D#, F#, [B], D#   5:6:8:10
[B], D#, F#, A#, B   8:10:12:15:16
F#, A#, [B], D#, F#   12:15:16:20:24
A#, [B], D#, F#, A#   15:16:20:24:30


C
G, [C], E, G   3:4:5:6
[C], E, G, A#, C   4:5:6:7:8
E, G, A#, [C], E   5:6:7:8:9:10
G, A#, [C], D, E, G   6:7:8:9:10:12
A#, [C], D, E, G, A#   7:8:9:10:12:14
[C], D, E, G, A#, B, C   8:9:10:12:14:15:16
D, E, G, A#, B, [C], D   9:10:12:14:15:16:18
G, A#, B, [C], D, E, G   12:14:15:16:18:20:24
A#, B, [C], D, E, G, A#   14:15:16:18:20:24:28
A#, B, [C], D, E, G#, A#   14:15:16:18:20:25:28
B, [C], D, E, G, A#   15:16:18:20:24:28
B, [C], D, E, G#, A#   15:16:18:20:25:28
[C], D, E, G# 16:18:20:25
```

C#
G#, [C#], D#, G# 6:8:9:12
[C#], D#, G#, C# 8:9:12:16

D
[D], F, F#, A# 16:19:20:25

D#
A#, [D#], E, A# 12:16:17:24
A#, [D#], A# 3:4:6

Chapter Eleven
Eagle 53 Chords

For a long time I had thought that if every note in a chord "goes with" every other note in the chord, according to the list on pages 39 to 41, then the chord should be good. Not any more. If the overall strength (or periodicity) value of a chord is less than 0.4 then the chord is, for me, illegal (see page 38).

There are very many chords where any and every pair of notes makes a good harmony interval but the overall strength is less than 0.4. I won't use these chords.

In Eagle 53, if the the first note (1/1 or 0 cents) is E then major chords are available on E, F, G, A, B and C.

Minor chords occur on E, G#, A, B, C# and D#. All of the intervals in these major and minor chords are within 1.4 cents of just.

A six note E minor chord on a guitar is close to 10:15:20:24:30:40. If you omit the 24 and divide the other numbers by 5 you get 2:3:4:6:8. This chord has only two pitch classes (E and B, E on 2, 4 and 8 and B on 3 and 6), the G note is gone. Two musicians I am acquainted with described this 2:3:4:6:8 chord as 'empty' and 'hollow' but I love it and have no qualms about using it in my music. I prefer it to the 10:15:20:24:30:40 superset minor chord. The 2:3:4:6:8 chord is a lush chord: it has a strength value of 2.75 (greater than 0.75) and is strongly rooted (contains a 2 in the IRC). The 10:15:20:24:30:40 minor chord is not lush: it has a strength value of 0.633 (less than 0.75) and is not strongly rooted, it does not contain a 1, 2, 4, 8 or 16 in its IRC.

There are no major or minor chords available on F#, A# and D. Luckily there are *lush chords* available on F# and D. They look like this... 4:5:8:10:16. That is F#,A#,F#,A#,F# on F# and D,F#,D,F#,D on D.

These 4:5:8:10:16 chords have only two pitch classes which some musicians will object to but I like them and have no problem using them.

There is no lush chord on A# but this chord is available... 7:10:14:20:28. Note that 20/7 does not occur in my list of good harmony intervals but it turns out that the two notes involved make an interval that is within 8.474 cents of 17/6 which does occur in my list of good harmony intervals.

Some chords are more suitable for pianos or keyboards and others are more suitable for guitars (fretted for Eagle 53). On piano I recommend...

E major, E minor, 2:3:4:6:8 and 4:5:8:10:16

F major, 2:3:4:6:8 and 4:5:8:10:16

F# 4:5:8:10:16

G major, 2:3:4:6:8 and 4:5:8:10:16

G# minor and 2:3:4:6:8

A major, minor, 2:3:4:6:8 and 4:5:8:10:16

A# 7:10:14:20:28

B major, minor, 2:3:4:6:8 and 4:5:8:10:16

C major, 2:3:4:6:8 and 4:5:8:10:16

C# minor and 2:3:4:6:8

D 4:5:8:10:16

D# minor and 2:3:4:6:8

On guitars fretted for Eagle 53 I recommend...

E major (2:3:4:5:6:8), open or otherwise

F major (2:3:4:5:6:8)

F# 4:5:8:10

G major (2:3:4:5:6:8) or Open G (4:5:6:8:10:16)

G# minor (10:15:20:24:30:40) or 2:3:4:6

A major or minor, open or otherwise or 2:3:4:6 or 4:5:8:10

A# 7:10:14:20 (20/7 ≈ 17/6)

B major or minor or 2:3:4:6 or 4:5:8:10

C major (open or otherwise) or 2:3:4:6 or 4:5:8:10

C# minor or 2:3:4:6

D 2:4:5:8 (D, D, F#, D) or 6:10:12:15 (D, B, D, F# open chord)

D# minor or 2:3:4:6

Note that the D chords in Eagle 53 function in a very different way to D chords in 12TET. D over the E below it in 12TET makes a 16/9 interval whereas D over the E below it in Eagle 53 makes a 9/5 interval.

Sometimes a 2:3:4:6:8 or 4:5:8:10 chord will work better than a 2:3:4:5:6:8 chord on the same note. More on this in the next chapter.

Chapter Twelve
Composition

Here are some rules that I follow when I compose. The first thing I do is establish what I call 'the melodic base'. In Eagle 53 most of the notes, over any range (e.g. seven octaves), pair nicely with each other (melodically) but there are a small number of melodic intervals that I deem to be sour. I want to avoid these sour melodic intervals.

Here is an example. Assume E is on 1/1. If I play an A note then the D note just above it sounds good to me. However, if I play a D note then the A note just above it sounds sour to me.

So when I compose I want every note I play to pair nicely (melodically) with every other note I play. So I have to set up a 'melodic base'. Here are the rules for choosing and avoiding notes (where E is on 1/1). When you choose, say, an A note, you are not choosing *all* the A notes from lower to higher, just the A note that corresponds to one pitch or frequency.

If you choose an A, avoid D 7 notes below it and D 19 notes below it.

If you choose an A#, avoid F 7 notes above it and F 19 notes above it.

B is always good.

If you choose a C, avoid C# 1 note above it.

If you choose a C#, avoid C 1 note below it and F# 7 notes below it and F# 19 notes below it.

If you choose a D, avoid D# 1 note above it and A 7 notes above it and A 19 notes above it.

If you choose a D#, avoid D 1 note below it.

E is always good.

If you choose an F, avoid A# 7 notes below it and and A# 19 notes below it.

If you choose an F#, avoid C# 7 notes above it and C# 19 notes above it.

If you choose a G, avoid G# 1 note above it.

If you choose a G#, avoid G 1 note below it.

You could keep going until all available notes are either chosen or to be avoided. The E and B notes are always good. Every E and B note pairs nicely, melodically, with every other note over any range. Note that these rules apply to my Eagle 53 tuning and do *not* apply to 12 Tone Equal Temperament.

If you play a piano or keyboard you could place green stickers on the chosen keys and red stickers on the keys to avoid. If you play guitar then you could draw a diagram of the fretboard (or scan and print the diagram on the back cover of this book) and draw circles to indicate the chosen notes and draw Xs to indicate the notes to avoid. Obviously on a guitar some notes occur more than once (e.g. the 5th fret on the bottom E string produces the same note as the open A string).

Ideally every chord must be good according to my criteria *and* every note in every chord played must belong to the melodic base. A less strict approach (but perhaps acceptable) would allow *any* strongly rooted chord (contains a 1, 2, 4, 8 or 16 in the IRC) that has a strength value >= 0.4 as long as the root note is part of the melodic base (i.e. one or more notes in the chord may not belong to the melodic base but that's okay as long as the root note note *does* belong). Melodically, if you stick to the chosen notes you can't play a sour note (if I'm right).

Chapter Thirteen
Eagle 53 Guitar

If the frequency of the first note in Eagle 53 (corresponding to 1/1) is x then the relative frequencies of the subsequent notes (over a four octave range) are...

1x, 1.06758x, 1.12491x, 1.20093x, 1.24898x, 1.33339x, 1.405x, 1.49994x, 1.6013x, 1.66538x, 1.80132x, 1.8734x, 2x, 2.13515x, 2.24982x, 2.40186x, 2.49797x, 2.66677x, 2.80999x, 2.99988x, 3.2026x, 3.33075x, 3.60265x, 3.7468x, 4x, 4.27031x, 4.49965x, 4.80372x, 4.99594x, 5.33354x, 5.61998x, 5.99976x, 6.40521x, 6.66151x, 7.20529x, 7.49361x, 8x, 8.54061x, 8.99929x, 9.60743x, 9.99187x, 10.6671x, 11.24x, 11.9995x, 12.8104x, 13.323x, 14.4106x, 14.9872x, 16x.

These relative frequencies can be used to work out where to position the frets on a guitar built for Eagle 53. If the tonic (1/1) is E, and the guitar is tuned EADGBE then an Eagle 53 fretboard looks like this...

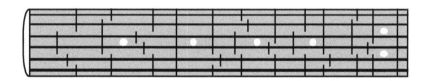

Below are lists of how far each fret should be from the nut for each of the 12 keys of E53. If the guitar will be tuned EADGBE (and E is the tonic) then the lists of fret positions for each string correspond to Key 1, Key 6, Key 11, Key 4, Key 8 and Key 1 again. The y below corresponds to the scale length of the guitar which is the distance from the nut to the saddle on the lightest string. So if the scale length is 60 cm (around 24 inches) then y would be 60 cm.

Key 1 (E) 0.0632991y, 0.111041y, 0.167311y, 0.199349y, 0.25003y, 0.288254y, 0.333307y, 0.375508y, 0.399535y, 0.444852y, 0.466212y, 0.5y, 0.53165y, 0.555521y, 0.583656y, 0.599675y, 0.625015y, 0.644127y, 0.666654y

Key 2 (F) 0.0509683y, 0.111041y, 0.145244y, 0.199349y, 0.240157y, 0.288254y, 0.333307y, 0.358958y, 0.407337y, 0.43014y, 0.466212y, 0.5y, 0.525484y, 0.555521y, 0.572622y, 0.599675y, 0.620078y, 0.644127y, 0.666654y

Key 3 (F#) 0.063299y, 0.0993387y, 0.15635y, 0.199349y, 0.25003y, 0.297502y, 0.324531y, 0.375508y, 0.399535y, 0.437544y, 0.473147y, 0.5y, 0.531649y, 0.549669y, 0.578175y, 0.599675y, 0.625015y, 0.648751y, 0.662265y

Key 4 (G) 0.0384751y, 0.0993388y, 0.145244y, 0.199349y, 0.25003y, 0.278885y, 0.333307y, 0.358958y, 0.399536y, 0.437544y, 0.466212y, 0.5y, 0.519238y, 0.549669y, 0.572622y, 0.599675y, 0.625015y, 0.639442y, 0.666654y

Key 5 (G#) 0.0632991y, 0.111041y, 0.167311y, 0.22002y, 0.25003y, 0.30663y, 0.333307y, 0.375508y, 0.415038y, 0.444852y, 0.479993y, 0.5y, 0.53165y, 0.555521y, 0.583656y, 0.61001y, 0.625015y, 0.653315y, 0.666654y

Key 6 (A) 0.0509682y, 0.111041y, 0.167311y, 0.199349y, 0.259774y, 0.288254y, 0.333307y, 0.375508y, 0.407337y, 0.444852y, 0.466212y, 0.5y, 0.525484y, 0.555521y, 0.583656y, 0.599675y, 0.629887y, 0.644127y, 0.666654y

Key 7 (A#) 0.0632991y, 0.122591y, 0.15635y, 0.22002y, 0.25003y, 0.297502y, 0.341969y, 0.375508y, 0.415038y, 0.437544y, 0.473147y, 0.5y, 0.53165y, 0.561296y, 0.578175y, 0.61001y, 0.625015y, 0.648751y, 0.670985y

Key 8 (B) 0.0632991y, 0.0993387y, 0.167311y, 0.199349y, 0.25003y, 0.297502y, 0.333307y, 0.375508y, 0.399535y, 0.437544y, 0.466212y, 0.5y, 0.53165y, 0.549669y, 0.583656y, 0.599675y, 0.625015y, 0.648751y, 0.666654y

Key 9 (C) 0.0384751y, 0.111041y, 0.145244y, 0.199349y, 0.25003y, 0.288254y, 0.333307y, 0.358958y, 0.399535y, 0.43014y, 0.466212y, 0.5y, 0.519238y, 0.555521y, 0.572622y, 0.599675y, 0.625015y, 0.644127y, 0.666654y

Key 10 (C#) 0.0754697y, 0.111041y, 0.167311y, 0.22002y, 0.259774y, 0.30663y, 0.333307y, 0.375508y, 0.407337y, 0.444852y, 0.479993y, 0.5y, 0.537735y, 0.555521y, 0.583656y, 0.61001y, 0.629887y, 0.653315y, 0.666654y

Key 11 (D) 0.0384751y, 0.0993387y, 0.15635y, 0.199349y, 0.25003y, 0.278885y, 0.324531y, 0.358958y, 0.399535y, 0.437544y, 0.459185y, 0.5y, 0.519238y, 0.549669y, 0.578175y, 0.599675y, 0.625015y, 0.639442y, 0.662265y

Key 12 (D#) 0.0632991y, 0.122591y, 0.167311y, 0.22002y, 0.25003y, 0.297502y, 0.333307y, 0.375508y, 0.415038y, 0.437544y, 0.479993y, 0.5y, 0.53165y, 0.561296y, 0.583656y, 0.61001y, 0.625015y, 0.648751y, 0.666654y

Chapter Fourteen
Keyboard Chord Finder

I have an idea for an electronic keyboard that has a light above each key to facilitate finding strong chords. When a key is pressed then all of the other keys that pair well (in harmony) with the pressed key will be indicated by a light above them. When I say *pair well*, I mean that the two notes played will be within +/- 8.474 cents of any just interval that has a value greater than 0.4 using the $2/x + 2/y$ formula.

So after pressing the first key the second key pressed should be one of the keys indicated by a light. When the second key is pressed all the other keys that pair well with *both* the first and second keys will be indicated by a light (there will fewer lights at this stage). When a third key is chosen (must be indicated by a light) then all the other keys that pair well with all three keys already pressed will be indicated by lights, and so on until the desired number of notes is reached or no more lights occur.

Finally, when the desired chord is found the root note of the chord (which isn't always the lowest note) could be indicated with a light of another colour (see the chapter on harmony and chords for a method for identifying the root note of a chord). The strength value of the chord played could also be displayed on the keyboard. If the strength value is less than 0.4 then the chord is, for me, illegal.

Lights could be used for finding nice melodies as well as chords. See the chapter on composition.

Chapter Fifteen
For the Record

I propose a naming system for Eagle 53 instruments. In 12 Tone Equal Temperament the A notes have set frequencies or pitches. So standard A notes have frequencies of 55Hz, 110Hz, 220Hz, 440Hz, 880Hz or any notes that are octaves lower or higher than these. Similarly the E notes have fixed frequencies of 41.2Hz, 82.4Hz, 164.8Hz, 329.6Hz and so on.

With my Eagle 53 tuning the notes are named similarly to 12TET but they do not correspond to fixed frequencies, they are variable. The notes of Eagle 53 over a one octave range are very close to the following just notes...

1/1, 16/15, 9/8, 6/5, 5/4, 4/3, 7/5, 3/2, 8/5, 5/3, 9/5, 15/8, 2/1.

The first note, 1/1, could be set to any desired frequency (say it's 100Hz for this example). The second note will be (approximately) 100Hz by 16/15. The third note will be (approximately) 100Hz by 9/8 and so on.

I have decided to name 1/1, "E". 16/15 is "F". 9/8 is "F#" (or Gb). 6/5 is "G", and so on, similar to the 12TET system. But these names do not correspond to fixed frequencies or pitches, they can be assigned any pitches you want. On my Eagle guitar the bottom E string is tuned to the standard 12TET 'E' (82.4Hz if I remember correctly). So my "Eagle E" is tuned to "Equal E" if you see what I mean. I could tune all the strings up a standard 100 cents semitone and then my "Eagle E" would be tuned to "Equal F". I could tune my Eagle E down a semitone and then my "Eagle E" would be tuned to "Equal D#".

In other words with my Eagle E, F, F#, G, G#, A etc. I could choose any note from standard 12TET and that will be how my Eagle E is tuned and all the other Eagle notes will be tuned relative to this chosen pitch. Why do it this way?

Imagine playing a composition on a keyboard tuned to Eagle 53 and the E key (1/1) is tuned to "Equal E". If you want to play the same tune in, say, Equal G and you retuned the keyboard so that "Eagle E" is now tuned to "Equal G" and is located on the physical white G key you will have to learn a lot of new chord and scale shapes, many of which didn't exist in the initial tuning. This is because Eagle 53 is not an equal tuning, the distances between adjacent notes varies quite a bit.

Put simply keeping the Eagle 1/1 on just one key (the 'E' key) vastly reduces the number of chord and scale shapes you would need to memorize. If "Eagle E" is implemented on any other physical key (other than a white E key) on a keyboard (e.g. F#) a whole new set of chord and scale shapes need to be learned which complicates matters a lot. It's much simpler to always have "Eagle E" on the physical E key. If you want to play the same piece in another key, choose any 12TET pitch you want for "Eagle E" and all the other notes must be tuned up or down according to Eagle 53 and 1/1 will always be on the physical E white key.

To implement this idea I propose a switch on electronic keyboards whereby every note on the instrument can be simultaneously tuned up or down by 1 or 2 or 3 or 4 or 5 or 6 standard 100 cents semitones. The default tuning could be Eagle 53 where "Eagle E" is tuned to "Equal E" on the physical E white key and all the other notes are tuned according to the Eagle 53 tuning.

Electric or amplified guitars could use a pedal that shifts the pitches of the notes played up or down by 1 or 2 or 3 or 4 or 5 or 6 standard semitones but this may not be practical if the player can hear both the physical guitar and the retuned notes coming out of a speaker at the same time. Headphones might work here.

Chapter Sixteen
Resources and Links

For discussion on microtonal music and tuning theory go to...

www.facebook.com/groups/xenharmonic2
or
www.facebook.com/groups/497105067092502

There is a microtonal encyclopaedia at...

tonalsoft.com

For music in my own Blue, Raven and Eagle tunings (mostly by Chris Vaisvil) and more information go to...

www.johnsmusic7.com

I have my own forum for discussing Eagle 53...

www.facebook.com/groups/eagletuning

Afterword

As I said in the introduction, my formulas and cut off points for melody and harmony intervals might turn out to be inaccurate or wrong but even if they did, looking at it from every angle, I still think that the Eagle 53 tuning is unbeatable for my intents and purposes and chosen criteria. This is what I set out to find back in 1995.

I don't like beats/beating and I find beating to be noticeable in the 6/5 (minor third) interval and more noticeable in narrower intervals (excluding the unison, 1/1) on my Eagle 53 guitar. If I were to be very strict I wouldn't allow any intervals between 8.474 cents and 377.8 cents (377.8c is a just 5/4, 386.3c, tempered narrower by 8.474c). Noticeable beating also occurs in intervals where the first overtone of the lower note and the fundamental of the higher note makes an interval between 8.474 cents and 377.8 cents. Avoiding these beating intervals would preclude the 2:3:4:5:6:8 major chord (5:6 would be illegal) and *all* minor chords (which contain a 6/5 interval). I am not *banning* these beating intervals but I intend to compose some music in the future that avoids them. This is where the 2:3:4:5:8, 2:3:4:6:8 and 4:5:8:10:16 chords become very useful. They are strong, strongly rooted, no obvious beating and all the intervals in the chords (where they occur) are within 1.4 cents of just in Eagle 53. At least one of these three chords occur on every note in Eagle 53 except the tritone (if 1/1 is on E then the tritone is A# or 7/5). A 7:10:14:20:28 chord occurs on A#. 20/7≈17/6. The 2:3:4:6:8 and 4:5:8:10:16 chords have only two pitch classes but that doesn't bother me at all, I love these chords.

I have six other books in print at the time of writing...

-The Eagle 53 Guitarist Lush Chords-
-The Eagle 53 Guitarist Jazz Chords-

-The Eagle 53 Pianist-
-Eagle 53 Jazz Chords-

These are all available on Amazon. Go to my website for descriptions of the books and links to Amazon...

www.johnsmusic7.com

If you want to email me there will either be a contact form or an email address at the bottom of my main web page. If my books start to sell well then I imagine I will get a lot of emails and may not have time to respond to all of them. I have my own Facebook forum at..

www.facebook.com/groups/eagletuning

The equipment I used in my research included...
Two old Apple iMacs, one running OS 9 and the other running OS X 10.4.11. and a newer 2014 Apple iMac
A PSR 275 Yamaha midi keyboard.

The software I used included...
AppleWorks (word processing and drawing)
Real Time Tuner by Wm. S. Cooper (tuning software)
PitchFork PPC by Tom Erbe (used for testing sine wave intervals)
CodeWarrior by Metrowerks (programming software)
Xcode by Apple Computer, Inc. (programming software)

The books I referred to included...
The Just Intonation Primer by David B. Doty
The Guitar Handbook by Ralph Denyer

A shorter, older and cheaper ebook version of this book is available on Amazon. It is called: Eagle 53 Musical Tuning.

Enjoy the Music

John O'Sullivan

1st July, 2021

Lightning Source UK Ltd.
Milton Keynes UK
UKHW020839040721
386608UK00002B/23